P9-DFH-035

SIMPLY GLUTEN FREE

5 Ingredient Cookbook

Fast, Fresh & Simple!

FEATURING 15-MINUTE RECIPES

BLUEBERRY
PANCAKES
PAGE 23

Contents

Contributors

HALLIE KLECKER, a cookbook author and recipe developer, is the creator of the gluten-free recipe website Daily Bites (*dailybitesblog.com*), where she shares her passion for health and wellness. In her cookbooks, *Super Healthy Cookies* and *The Pure Kitchen*, she transforms clean, unprocessed ingredients into delicious meals and treats.

JENNIFER PEÑAS is The Cocktail Lady who was given (and completed!) the challenge of finding, making, trying and blogging about a new cocktail every day for a year. You can find her at *cocktail365.blogspot.com*.

PORK ROAST
WITH
CIDER GRAVY
PAGE 125

When it comes to gluten-free recipes, one of the most intimidating factors for many people is looking at a long list of ingredients. Right off the bat, the recipe appears complicated, and the thought of all that shopping can feel overwhelming. The truth is, great food doesn't have to be complicated or contain 20-plus items. You can create delicious dishes with just a handful of the right ingredients.

This book contains recipes from breakfast to dinner, cocktails to desserts—all of which contain just five ingredients, not including water, oil, salt and pepper. It has been one of my life's missions to prove that cooking and eating gluten-free can be elegantly simple and, of course, delicious. With these easy recipes, I hope to show that you can spend less time shopping and cooking and more time enjoying your life and the food that fits your lifestyle.

EDITOR-IN-CHIEF
SIMPLY GLUTEN FREE

Gluten-Free 101

Learn what gluten is, what it isn't and what you can do to avoid it easily at every meal.

What is Gluten?

Gluten is a protein found in many grains, including wheat, barley and rye—which means you'll find it in items as diverse as bread, pasta and beer.

Gluten is what makes baked goods stay together and causes gravies and sauces to thicken. It also adds elasticity to foods—it is what helps bread dough rise and pizza dough stretch. Most people would consider these qualities desirable. For people with celiac disease or gluten sensitivity, however, ingesting gluten is akin to eating just a tiny bit of rat poison. It won't kill them right away, but the long-term effects can be very detrimental. Their bodies perceive gluten in the same way they would rat poison—as a toxin.

Why Go Gluten-Free?

At first, the idea of a gluten-free diet might seem daunting. But for people with celiac disease or gluten intolerance, there's little alternative if they want to regain and maintain good health. This section will arm you with the information you need to begin your journey to vitality and good health with ease, even if you share your kitchen with people who do not follow a gluten-free diet.

Celiac disease and gluten intolerance are autoimmune diseases that damage the small intestine, causing a range of symptoms, including but not limited to, chronic intestinal problems, migraine headaches, infertility, chronic anemia, obesity, arthritis, memory loss, psoriasis, eczema, irritable bowel syndrome, low thyroid (hypothyroidism), chronic fatigue syndrome, type 1 or type 2 diabetes, autism and fibromyalgia. If left untreated, celiac disease can be fatal.

The simple and unfortunate fact is that there are no known cures for celiac disease or gluten intolerance. The only treatment is to fully commit to a gluten-free diet. On the flip side, committing to a diet without gluten can restore good health and improve the quality of your life—a payoff well worth all your efforts!

It is vitally important to understand that any amount of gluten can cause symptoms to occur. Lessening gluten intake does no good: You must go completely gluten-free, even down to the minute quantity of parts-per-million in a food product. It is generally accepted that a food has to contain less than 20 ppm—that's 20 little particles out of one million—of gluten for a food to be safely gluten-free.

After more than 20 years of living gluten-free, it is second nature to me. I do, however, recall the initial confusion and frustration following my diagnosis. I love to cook and eat good food, and I hate diets! So the challenge became how to live my lifestyle around my gluten intolerance. I'll teach you how you can accomplish that seemingly daunting task in today's world of food.

What Can You Eat?

Some foods are more obvious than others when it comes to steering clear of gluten. The lists on the following pages will help you determine what is safe, what is unsafe and what is questionable. Use these guides to put together a custom shopping list of your favorite safe, gluten-free foods.

Safe Foods

Baking Soda

Beans & Lentils
Dried, canned, soybeans and tofu (check labels for mixed and baked beans)

Chocolate
Milk, semisweet, bittersweet and unsweetened (check labels for add-ins)

Coffee
Check labels if flavored

Condiments
Mayonnaise, ketchup, most mustard (check labels), pickles, olives, hot sauce, salad dressings (check labels), Lea and Perrin's Worcestershire sauce (in the U.S.), salsa and Wright's Liquid Smoke

Cream of Tartar

Dairy
Milk, buttermilk, cream, half-and-half, cheeses, butter (check labels of unsalted, whipped and light varieties) and yogurt (check labels if flavored)

Eggs

Fish & Seafood
All safe as long as not marinated or breaded

Fruit
Fresh, frozen, canned and pure fruit juices

Gums
Acacia, carrageenan, carob bean, cellulose, guar, locust bean and xanthan

Lactose

Lecithin

Meat
All fresh varieties safe as long as not marinated or breaded (check labels on deli meats)

Nuts
Fresh and roasted (check labels on nut butters, nut flours and canned nuts for flour or coatings)

Oils
Vegetable, nut, coconut, olive and seed; margarines and shortenings

Pectin

Poultry
All safe as long as not marinated, injected or breaded (check labels on turkeys and deli varieties)

Rice
All varieties are safe unless they are mixed with gluten flavorings or cross-contaminated

Seeds
Fresh, roasted, butters (check labels of canned and bottled varieties for flour or coatings)

Spices
Whole or ground (check labels on mixed spices)

Sweeteners
Cane, beet, coconut, brown, turbinado, agave syrup, cane syrup, corn syrup, glucose, honey, fructose, maple syrup, molasses, stevia, aspartame, erythritol, maltitol, maltose, sorbitol, sucralose and xylitol

Tea
(Check labels if flavored)

Vegetables
Fresh, frozen or canned

Vinegars
Rice, rice wine and distilled (including red, white, balsamic and red wine) (Note: Malt vinegar is not safe)

Yeast

Unsafe Foods

Barley
Barley Enzyme
Barley Extract
Barley Grass
Barley Malt
Barley Pearls
Bleached Flour
Bolted Flour
Bran
Bread Flour
Bromated Flour
Bulgur
Bulgur Wheat
Cake Flour
Chapati Flour
Couscous
Durum
Einkorn
Emmer
Enriched Flour
Farina
Farro
Gluten Flour
Graham
Hordeum Vulgare
Hydrolyzed Wheat
Instant Flour
Kamut
Malt
Malt Vinegar
Matzo
Organic Flour
Pastry Flour
Seitan
Self-Rising Flour
Spelt
Semolina
Tabbouleh
Triticale
Udon
Vital Wheat Gluten
Wheat
Wheat Berry
Wheat Bran
Wheat Flour
Wheat Germ
Wheat Oil
Wheat Protein
Wheat Starch
White Flour

Questionable Foods

Artificial Extracts

Asian Sauces
  Soy, tamari, etc.

Bacon

Baking Powder

Barbecue Sauces

Bouillon Cubes

Brown Rice Syrup

Caramel Color

Dextrin

Fillers

Flavorings
  Natural and artificial

Gravies

Hydrolyzed or Texturized Plant
  or Vegetable Protein

Imitation Bacon

Imitation Seafood

Licorice

Meat Substitutes

Miso

Modified Food Starch

Mono- and Dyglycerides

Most Mustards

MSG
  GF if from U.S.

Multi-Grain Products

Mustard Powder

Prepared Broths

Prepared Meats

Breaded, floured, injected or
marinated

Prepared Soups

Prepared Stews

Processed Meats
  Deli meats

Sausages

Seasonings
  Blended spices

Vegetable Gums

Common Foods That Contain Gluten

Baked Goods
  Biscuits, cakes, cookies, muffins,
  pies and pastries

Beer
  Unless certified gluten-free

Breads
  Buns, multigrain, pita, pizza
  crust, potato, pumpernickel, rye,
  sourdough, wheat and white

Breakfast Foods
  Bagels, breakfast bars, cereals,
  doughnuts, pancakes and waffles

Crackers
  Butter, cheese, graham, melba toast,
  rye, saltines and wheat

Pasta
  All shapes, orzo and rice mixed with
  pasta

Miscellaneous
  Breadcrumbs, croutons, flour
  tortillas and communion wafers

Unexpected Enemies

Food items are not the only sources of gluten to be aware of. Vitamins, medications and cosmetics can all contain small traces of gluten that can put a halt to your recovery. Check labels or call manufacturers to be sure about a product. Nothing can be as disheartening as thinking you are sticking to a completely gluten-free diet, only to find out a hidden source is slowly counteracting your hard work.

Gluten-Free Grains, Flours & Starches

Amaranth

Arrowroot

Bean Flours

Buckwheat

Cassava

Chestnut

Chickpea

Corn

Glutinous Rice

Millet

Montina

Nut Flours

Oats
  Only if certified

Pea

Potato

Quinoa

Rice

Sorghum

Soy

Sweet Rice

Tapioca

Taro

Teff

Prepping Your Kitchen

Learn how to cleanse your pantry and keep it gluten-free all year round.

Cross-Contamination

One of the major concerns for those on a gluten-free diet is how to avoid cross-contamination. A product can have only up to 20 ppm of gluten to be considered safe for a gluten-free diet. This means that even a tiny crumb of traditional bread might make you sick, depending on your level of sensitivity.

Now, I'm not trying to scare you—just inform you of what to be aware of, so you can try to avoid being "glutened" from cross-contamination.

Some foods, such as oats, are gluten-free themselves; however, due to the processing of these foods, they are often cross-contaminated. This occurs when one type of food is processed on the same equipment as another, resulting in gluten from one food being transferred to another.

Cross-contamination is also a concern in the kitchen, whether you're home or at a restaurant that serves food containing gluten. For example, if someone baking with gluten flour and sugar measures the flour first, then sticks the same measuring cup in the sugar, it is no longer gluten-free. Measuring cups and spoons should be washed before they are dipped into another canister if products with gluten are being used. The best solution for your own home is to get each canister its own scooper.

But you don't always have control over kitchens, particularly when you're in a restaurant, so you should always ask questions and inform the chef of your needs. If you still don't feel you can trust the situation, try another restaurant or ask if there are pre-packaged, gluten-free options. Leaving the cooking up to someone else might make you uneasy at first, but you learn to find trusted restaurants that will ensure you have a safe dining experience. As long as you are aware cross-contamination is a possibility and you do your best to prevent it, you should be fine.

Eliminating the Enemy

Now that you have a better idea of what you can and cannot eat, it is time to purge!

Go through your refrigerator, pantry, spice cabinet—even your vitamin cabinet—and get rid of anything that contains gluten. Also go through your appliances and kitchenware and do the same.

My best advice is to set aside ample time. Schedule a few hours when you can get the job done all at once, and do so as soon as possible. Getting rid of unsafe foods will make it easier for you to throw a meal together without much thought or effort because you won't have to stop to read labels.

Before you start the purge, make sure you have plenty of containers or plastic bags on hand to store your pantry items, along with a marker you can use to label them. This is especially important if you share a household with people who eat gluten.

You should start by removing all the food from your fridge, pantry and spice cabinets. Then, sort it into three categories: safe, unsafe and uncertain.

Safe foods are ones you know are gluten-free. Unsafe foods are the ones you know are not gluten-free. If you are making your household completely gluten-free, these foods can be thrown out, given away or donated. If you share a household with people who eat gluten, put things like flour, cereals and baking mixes into non-porous containers to prevent cross-contamination. Even an open cereal box of gluten cereal can cause cross-contamination. It is important for gluten-eaters to store gluten products appropriately, so you do not become ill.

Additionally, if you live with gluten-eaters, you should keep in mind that sharing condiments is a bad idea. If a gluten-eater spreads some jam on toast, then sticks the knife back into the jar, the "safe" jam has been contaminated. Put butter, jam, mustard, mayonnaise and anything else that has been used by gluten-eaters in the unsafe section of your kitchen.

Foods you are not certain about will require a little research. You can go online and search whether theses foods contain gluten, or you can contact the manufacturer. When in doubt, consider it unsafe.

Be sure to purge the medicine cabinets and your cosmetics, as well. Sort through these just as you did with the food items. You will likely have many items in the uncertain category, which might require a few phone calls to your pharmacist, doctor or product manufacturers.

Creating a Safe Space

Once you have sorted the food, it is time to clean the refrigerator and pantry. Gluten is a tiny molecule—and a sticky one at that. It sticks and clings to things long after the offending food item has been removed. Clean your refrigerator, pantry,

spice cabinet and medicine cabinet thoroughly—disinfectant wipes work well for this.

After you have cleaned everything, divide the real estate—if you share your household with gluten-eaters, that is. Set aside some space in the fridge and pantry that is strictly a gluten-free zone. If possible, have your gluten-free shelves higher than the non-gluten-free shelves. It is possible for some flour or other food particles to drift down onto your gluten-free foods, especially if they are not properly sealed and stored.

Once you have divided the space, put away your food. If you keep foods with gluten, transfer them into non-porous containers and label them. Mark contaminated condiments accordingly.

Once the food is taken care of, take a minute to look over your appliances and equipment. The rule of thumb is that non-porous materials such as glass, metal and Pyrex are fine. But porous storage, cooking and baking materials such as plastic, vinyl and wood will need to be replaced.

The toaster and bread maker are the most obvious appliances that will be contaminated with gluten. If you initially cannot afford to buy a new toaster, you can purchase toaster bags online. You can place your gluten-free bread into these, then put the bags into the toaster. If you make your own bread with a bread maker, unfortunately you will need to replace your old one. Additionally, if your blender has a rubber gasket, you will need to either replace the blender or the rubber gasket.

Non-stick skillets and pans with scratches are not safe because the gluten gets into those scratches and stays put. If it makes you feel better, the coating on non-stick cookware can be toxic if scratched, so they should be replaced, regardless. If it is too big of an expense to replace all your cookware, then buy one skillet of the most useful size (8 or 9 inches) to cook with until you can replace the others.

Cutting boards are another hot bed for hidden gluten. Manufacturers make colored vinyl cutting boards that are very inexpensive, and the color will easily identify the gluten-free boards, so you won't have to label them.

Wooden, vinyl and plastic utensils should not be used. Again, you can start with one all-purpose utensil, like a silicone spatula, until you eventually build up your new supply.

If you share your kitchen with gluten-eaters, make sure they know which equipment to use and that they clean up well after making food that contains gluten.

After all offending food, medicines and cookware items have been removed or stored separately, clean your entire kitchen. Clean all the counters, shelves and doors with hot, soapy water or disinfectant wipes. This may seem like a lot of work, but when you are done, you will not only have a safe kitchen, but you will also have one that is extremely clean and well organized!

Embracing Gluten-Free Foods

Now that your kitchen is safe, clean and organized, you get to do the fun part: Stock up on foods you can comfortably eat and enjoy!

I always advise people new to gluten-free diets to stick with foods that are naturally gluten-free—beef, chicken, fish, fruits, vegetables, rice and potatoes. Not only does it help your body to heal your intestines by staying away from grains, but it also gives your taste buds a chance to adjust and your cravings to stop.

There are a number of gluten-free breads, cereals and cake mixes that are becoming more readily available and are clearly marked as gluten-free. But not all gluten-free baked goods and mixes are created equal. Some are much better than others, and some will suit your taste more than others. When you find a brand you particularly enjoy, make note of the brand for future purchases. There will be some initial trial and error when shopping, and processed gluten-free foods can be a little more expensive than non-safe foods—but that is just

another reason you should stick with naturally gluten-free foods in the beginning.

I can't stress enough the importance of reading labels! Any packaged or processed food needs to be checked to make sure there is no hidden gluten. Even meats from the deli can contain gluten, so never assume just because a food shouldn't contain gluten that it doesn't.

When buying cereals, make sure to check the labels to see if they contain wheat or other gluten ingredients—do not assume that because it is a rice- or corn-based cereal that offending ingredients have not been added. Many regular grocery stores now carry gluten-free cereals that clearly say "gluten-free" on the label.

Most foods can be found at a regular grocery store. However, many grains and mixes may need to be purchased from health food stores or online.

The very best way to avoid feeling deprived is to load up on safe foods you love to eat and to have a few special treats on hand. It is easier to resist a piece of pie if you have something else to enjoy that you love and know you can safely eat. What I have found most helpful in going gluten-free is changing the way I think. I no longer look at food in terms of what I can't eat, but what I can eat. And thanks to these quick and easy recipes, those dishes are as plentiful as they are diverse and delicious.

Simple Substitutions

Learn how to make your own gluten-free, all-purpose flour and avoid other possibly offensive foods while making everything from breakfast to dessert.

Gluten-Free, All-Purpose Flour

SERVINGS Makes 9 cups flour mix.

INGREDIENTS

4 ½	cups white rice flour
1 ½	cups sweet rice flour
2	cups potato starch (not potato flour)
1	cup tapioca flour (also known as tapioca starch)
4	teaspoons xanthan or guar gum

DIRECTIONS

In a large mixing bowl, slowly whisk together all the ingredients, making sure they are evenly distributed. For best results, use superfine or Asian (such as Erawan brand) white and sweet rice flours.

USING YOUR BLEND

Use as a cup-for-cup replacement for all-purpose wheat flour. For recipes calling for yeast, add ¾ teaspoon additional xanthan or guar gum per cup of flour. This recipe can easily be halved, doubled or tripled. Store in an airtight container. For maximum freshness, store in the freezer.

Other Replacements

Tailor the recipes in this book (or any of your own) to suit your personal dietary needs. These substitutions make eliminating allergens such as dairy and nuts easy.

1 cup milk

- 1 cup rice milk
- 1 cup coconut milk
- 1 cup hemp milk
- 1 cup almond milk (contains tree nuts)
- 1 cup soy milk
- 1 cup water
- 1 cup rice milk and 1 egg yolk for each cup (for full-fat milk)
- 1 cup water and 1 egg yolk for each cup (for full-fat milk)

1 cup buttermilk

- 1 cup plain rice, soy or hemp milk and 1 tablespoon lemon juice (allow to sit for 5 minutes to "sour" before using)
- 1 cup plain rice, soy or hemp milk and 1 tablespoon apple cider vinegar (allow to sit for 5 minutes to "sour" before using)
- 1 cup plain, dairy-free yogurt and 1 tablespoon lemon juice or vinegar (allow to sit for 5 minutes to "sour" before using)

1 cup yogurt

- 1 cup coconut milk yogurt
- 1 cup rice milk yogurt
- 1 cup soy milk yogurt
- 1 cup fruit puree
- 1 cup unsweetened applesauce

8 tablespoons butter (1 stick or ½ cup)

- 8 tablespoons Earth Balance Vegan Buttery Sticks
- 8 tablespoons Earth Balance Vegan Buttery Spread
- 8 tablespoons Spectrum Organic Shortening
- 8 tablespoons Fleischmann's Unsalted Margarine
- ⅓ cup organic canola oil
- ⅓ cup coconut oil
- ⅓ cup olive oil (not for baking)

1 cup cheese

- 1 cup vegan cheese alternative
- 1 cup Cheezly by VBites
- 1 cup Daiya Vegan Cheese (also soy-free)
- 1 cup Teese Vegan Cheese
- 1 cup Follow Your Heart Vegan Cheese
- 1 cup Parma! Vegan Parmesan (contains tree nuts)

8 ounces cream cheese

- 8 ounces Tofutti Better Than Cream Cheese
- 8 ounces Follow Your Heart Cream Cheese Alternative

1 cup sour cream

- 1 cup Tofutti Better Than Sour Cream
- 1 cup Follow Your Heart Sour Cream Alternative

1 cup heavy cream

- 1 cup So Delicious Creamer
- 1 cup full-fat coconut milk
- ⅔ cup dairy-free milk of choice and ⅓ cup melted margarine (or vegan butter, canola oil or coconut oil)
- 1 cup Silk or Mocha Mix Brand Soy Creamers

1 cup light cream

- 1 cup Silk or Mocha Mix Brand Soy Creamers
- 1 cup light coconut milk
- 1 cup So Delicious Creamer

1 egg

- 3 tablespoons unsweetened applesauce and 1 teaspoon baking powder
- 1 tablespoon flax meal and 3 tablespoons hot water (mix together and let sit for 5 minutes to set and become gel-like)
- 1½ teaspoons Ener-G Egg Replacer

and 2 tablespoons water or dairy-free milk (whisked until foamy)
- 1 teaspoon baking powder, 1½ tablespoons water and 1½ tablespoons oil
- 3 tablespoons mashed bananas
- 3 tablespoons fruit puree and 1 teaspoon baking powder
- 4 tablespoons pureed silken tofu (pureed in blender) and 1 teaspoon baking powder
- 3½ tablespoons prepared gelatin (following directions on box)

1 egg white

- 1 tablespoon plain agar powder and 1 tablespoon water (dissolve powder, beat and chill for 15 minutes, then beat again)

1 cup mayonnaise

- 1 cup Vegenaise (free of multiple allergens, vegan)
- 1 cup Spectrum Light Canola Mayonnaise (egg-free)
- 1 cup Mindful Mayo by Earth Balance (free of multiple allergens)

Nuts

Peanuts, cashews, almonds, walnuts, pecans, pine nuts, pistachios, etc.:

- Toasted coconut
- Sunflower seeds
- Pumpkin seeds
- Crushed cornflakes
- Crushed crispy rice cereal
- Crushed potato chips
- Perky's Crunchy Flax Cereal by Enjoy Life
- Perky's Crunchy Rice Cereal by Enjoy Life

1 cup nut butter

- 1 cup sunflower seed butter

1 cup corn syrup

- 1 cup honey
- 1 cup agave nectar
- 1 cup pure maple syrup

1 cup refined white or brown cane sugar

- 1 cup coconut palm sugar

A.M. Eats

These quick and simple recipes make preparing breakfast and brunch as easy as Sunday morning.

HONEY ALMOND
PANCAKES

USING THE MIX
Add 2 large eggs (or an equivalent amount of egg substitute) and 1 cup milk (or dairy-free milk) to 2 cups of basic pancake mix, then whisk. Ladle ¼ cup of batter onto a greased griddle heated to medium. Cook until the bottoms of the pancakes are brown and the surfaces have tiny bubbles, about 5 minutes. Flip and cook until brown, about 1 minute. Keep cooked pancakes warm in the oven while preparing the rest. This recipe yields 12 pancakes, best served warm.

BASIC PANCAKES

Basic Pancake Mix

SERVINGS Makes 6 cups of mix.

Gluten-free, Dairy-free, Egg-free, Nut-free, Refined Sugar-free, Soy-free, Vegan, Vegetarian

INGREDIENTS
4 ½   cups brown rice flour (preferably superfine)
1 ½   cups tapioca starch
3   tablespoons baking powder
1   tablespoon kosher or fine sea salt
1   cup non-hydrogenated vegetable shortening (preferably organic)

DIRECTIONS
1. In a large mixing bowl, whisk together brown rice flour, tapioca starch, baking powder and salt. Cut shortening into the dry ingredients until the mixture resembles fine crumbs.

2. Store the mixture in an airtight container in the refrigerator for up to 4 months. Use as you would store-bought pancake mix.

Apple Cinnamon Pancakes

SERVINGS Makes 8 to 10 pancakes.

Gluten-free, Egg-free, Nut-free, Soy-free, Vegetarian, Optionally Dairy-free, Optionally Vegan

INGREDIENTS
1 ¼   cups Basic Pancake Mix
¾   cup milk or dairy-free milk
4   tablespoons applesauce
1   teaspoon ground cinnamon
2   teaspoons sugar
    Grape-seed or vegetable oil, to cook

APPLE CINNAMON PANCAKES

DIRECTIONS
1. Preheat oven to 200 degrees F.

2. In a large mixing bowl, whisk together the pancake mix, milk, applesauce, cinnamon and sugar.

3. Heat a skillet or griddle over medium until a drop of water sprinkled on the pan sizzles immediately. Brush the pan with oil and heat for a few seconds.

4. Ladle a scant ¼ cup of pancake batter onto the pan for each pancake. Cook until the bottoms are golden brown, the edges look dry and the surface of the pancake has tiny bubbles, about 5 minutes. Flip and cook for another minute, or until the bottoms are brown. Keep cooked pancakes warm in the oven while preparing the rest. Serve warm.

Honey Almond Pancakes

SERVINGS Makes 10 to 12 pancakes.

Gluten-free, Grain-free, Dairy-free,
Refined Sugar-free, Soy-free, Vegetarian

INGREDIENTS

- 2 cups finely ground, blanched almond flour
- 3 large eggs
- ¾ cup water
- 2 tablespoons honey
- ½ teaspoon baking soda
- ½ teaspoon kosher or fine sea salt
  Grape-seed or vegetable oil, to cook

DIRECTIONS

1. Preheat oven to 200 degrees F.

2. In a large mixing bowl, whisk together the almond flour, eggs, water, honey, baking soda and salt.

3. Heat a skillet or griddle over medium-low until a drop of water sprinkled on the pan sizzles immediately. Brush the pan with oil and heat for a few seconds.

4. Ladle a scant ¼ cup of pancake batter onto the pan for each pancake. Cook until the bottoms are golden brown, the edges look dry and the surface of the pancake has tiny bubbles, about 5 minutes. Flip and cook for another 1 ½ to 2 minutes, or until the bottoms are golden brown and the pancakes feel firm to the touch. Keep cooked pancakes warm in the oven while preparing the rest. Serve warm.

Blueberry Pancakes

SERVINGS Makes 12 pancakes.

*Gluten-free, Nut-free, Soy-free, Vegetarian,
Optionally Egg-free, Optionally Dairy-free,
Optionally Vegan*

INGREDIENTS

2	cups Basic Pancake Mix
2	large eggs or an equivalent amount of egg substitute
1	cup milk or dairy-free milk
1	tablespoon sugar
	Grape-seed or vegetable oil, to cook
1 ½	cups fresh or thawed frozen blueberries

DIRECTIONS

1. Preheat oven to 200 degrees F.

2. In a large mixing bowl, whisk together the pancake mix, eggs, milk and sugar.

3. Heat a skillet or griddle over medium until a drop of water sprinkled on the pan sizzles immediately. Brush the pan with oil and heat for a few seconds.

4. Ladle a scant ¼ cup of pancake batter onto the pan for each pancake. Sprinkle about 2 tablespoons of blueberries on top of the batter. Cook until the bottoms are golden brown, the edges look dry and the surface of the pancake has tiny bubbles, about 5 minutes. Flip and cook for another minute, or until the bottoms are brown. Keep cooked pancakes warm in the oven while preparing the rest. Serve warm.

BANANA
PANCAKES

Peanut Butter and Banana Pancakes

SERVINGS Makes 12 pancakes.

Gluten-free, Grain-free, Refined Sugar-free, Soy-free, Vegetarian, Optionally Nut-free

INGREDIENTS

- 2 large, ripe bananas, peeled
- ½ cup peanut, almond, cashew or sunflower seed butter
- 2 large eggs
- 1 teaspoon baking powder
  Grape-seed or vegetable oil, to cook

DIRECTIONS

1. Preheat oven to 200 degrees F.

2. Mash the bananas in a large mixing bowl. Add the nut or seed butter, eggs and baking powder. Mix well.

3. Heat a skillet or griddle over medium-low until a drop of water sprinkled onto the pan sizzles immediately. Brush the pan with oil and heat for a couple of seconds.

4. Ladle ¼ cup of pancake batter onto the pan for each pancake. Cook until the bottoms are golden brown, the edges look dry and the surface of the pancake has tiny bubbles, about 5 minutes. Flip and cook for another minute, or until the bottoms are brown and the pancakes feel firm to the touch. Keep cooked pancakes warm in the oven while preparing the rest. Serve warm.

Lemon Ricotta Pancakes

SERVINGS Makes 12 pancakes.

Gluten-free, Grain-free, Nut-free, Refined Sugar-free, Soy-free, Vegetarian

INGREDIENTS

- 4 large eggs, separated
- 1 cup ricotta cheese, at room temperature
- 1 lemon, finely zested
- 1 pinch kosher or fine sea salt

DIRECTIONS

1. Beat the egg whites until stiff peaks form.

2. In a separate bowl, beat the ricotta cheese until smooth and creamy, about 2 minutes. Add the egg yolks, lemon zest and salt and beat until smooth and fluffy. Mix a scoop of egg whites into the yolk mixture to lighten it up some, then fold the yolk mixture into the whites.

3. Heat a griddle or skillet over medium until hot, then spray with gluten-free, nonstick cooking spray.

4. Scoop ⅓ cup of the mixture onto the pan for each pancake. (The batter will be really fluffy, so push it down with the bottom of the measuring cup to flatten it out a bit.) Cook over medium heat until golden brown on the bottom and cooked through, about 5 minutes. Flip and cook until pancakes are firm to touch, about 1 to 2 minutes.

Banana Pancakes

SERVINGS Makes 6 pancakes.

Gluten-free, Dairy-free, Nut-free, Refined Sugar-free, Soy-free, Vegetarian

INGREDIENTS

- 2 large, ripe bananas, peeled
- 4 large eggs
- 2 tablespoons pure maple syrup, plus more to serve
- ¼ teaspoon kosher or fine sea salt
- ¼ teaspoon baking powder
  Grape-seed or vegetable oil, to cook

DIRECTIONS

1. Mash the bananas in a mixing bowl. Add the eggs, 2 tablespoons maple syrup, salt and baking powder. Mix well.

2. Heat a little oil on a griddle or large skillet over medium. Ladle ⅓ cup of batter onto the pan for each pancake. Cook for 3 to 4 minutes, or until the pancakes look set and are starting to brown on the bottom. Flip and cook for another 3 minutes, or until golden brown.

3. Serve with maple syrup.

WHAT TO EXPECT
Lemon Ricotta Pancakes will be light and soufflé-like but deflate slightly if they sit for very long (they will still be delicious).

LEMON RICOTTA PANCAKES

Spanish Tortilla

SERVINGS Makes 6 main dish portions or 8 to 10 appetizer portions.

Gluten-free, Grain-free, Nut-free, Refined Sugar-free, Soy-free

INGREDIENTS

1	pound chorizo
1 ½	pounds baby Yukon Gold potatoes, sliced ⅛-inch thick
	Kosher or fine sea salt, to taste
	Freshly ground black pepper, to taste
1	small red onion, thinly sliced
12	large eggs, lightly beaten
4	ounces soft goat cheese, crumbled

DIRECTIONS

1. Remove the casings from the chorizo and place in a 12-inch nonstick, oven-proof skillet. Cook over medium heat until the sausage is fully cooked and has rendered its fat. With a slotted spoon, remove sausage and drain on paper towels.

2. Drain all but 2 tablespoons of the fat from the skillet, then add the potatoes and a large pinch of salt and pepper. Cook over medium heat for 10 minutes, gently stirring occasionally. (You want the potatoes to cook through but not brown. If they start to brown, reduce the heat.) Add the onions and cook for another 5 minutes, stirring occasionally, or until the onions are soft and the potatoes are fork tender and just starting to brown.

3. Reduce heat to low, pour in the chorizo, eggs and goat cheese, then gently pull the edges of the egg mixture to the center as it cooks so that any uncooked eggs run underneath.

4. Preheat broiler.

5. When the eggs are set around the edges and the mixture looks mostly cooked, place the skillet under the broiler for 2 to 3 minutes, or until the eggs are fully set and the tortilla is golden and slightly puffed.

6. Run a dinner knife around the edges of the tortilla to loosen it. Slide it onto a serving plate or cutting board. Cut into wedges and serve hot, warm, at room temperature or cold.

Creamed Eggs

SERVINGS Makes 4 portions.

Gluten-free, Nut-free, Refined Sugar-free, Soy-free, Vegetarian, Optionally Dairy-free

INGREDIENTS

- 5 tablespoons unsalted or dairy-free butter
- 5 tablespoons gluten-free, all-purpose flour
- 2 ½ cups milk or dairy-free milk
- 8 hard-boiled eggs, peeled and chopped
  Kosher or fine sea salt, to taste
  Freshly ground black pepper, to taste
- 8 slices gluten-free bread or 4 split gluten-free English muffins, toasted

DIRECTIONS

1. Melt butter in a large skillet over medium. Add flour and cook, whisking, for 1 minute. Whisk in the milk. Reduce heat to low and cook, stirring occasionally, until the mixture thickens, about 6 to 8 minutes. Stir in the eggs. Cook for 1 to 2 minutes, or until heated through. Season eggs with salt and pepper.

2. Serve eggs over toasted bread or English muffins.

Bacon and Asparagus Egg Soldiers

SERVINGS Makes 4 portions.

Gluten-free, Grain-free, Dairy-free,
Nut-free, Refined Sugar-free, Soy-free

INGREDIENTS
- 4   bacon slices
- 8   large asparagus spears, trimmed to about 5 inches long
- 4   soft-boiled eggs

DIRECTIONS

1. Preheat oven to 450 degrees F.

2. Cut bacon slices in half lengthwise and wrap one piece around each asparagus spear, covering all except the bud.

3. Place bacon-wrapped asparagus spears on a foil lined baking sheet and cook for 15 minutes, or until the bacon is brown and crispy. Briefly place spears on paper towels to soak up the excess grease and serve with soft boiled eggs.

UPPING THE ANTE

You can increase this recipe as much as you want, but when making a lot of crepes, be sure to regulate the heat. If the pan is too hot, the mixture will cook too quickly and the crepes will have holes in them. If the pan isn't hot enough, the crepes may be uneven in texture. I recommend using medium heat and spraying the pan with cooking spray between each batch.

Egg Crepes

Gluten-free, Grain-free, Dairy-free, Nut-free, Refined Sugar-free, Soy-free, Vegetarian

INGREDIENTS
- 1 large egg
- 1 tablespoon water
- 1 small pinch kosher or fine sea salt

DIRECTIONS

1. Combine the egg, water and salt with a fork until the mixture reaches a uniform consistency. Beat until fully combined but before the mixture becomes too frothy.

2. Heat a small skillet or crepe pan over medium.

3. Spray the pan lightly with gluten-free, nonstick cooking spray, then wipe with a paper towel so only a thin layer of cooking spray remains. Alternatively, you can wipe the pan with a small amount of oil or butter.

4. Return the pan to the heat for about 5 seconds, then ladle about 2 tablespoons (or enough to create a thin coating) of egg mixture into the pan. Rotate and evenly distribute the egg mixture. Cook about 2 minutes, or until the edges come away from the pan slightly and the bottom is browned. Carefully flip with a large silicone spatula and cook for about 1 minute. Slide crepe out of pan onto a plate. Continue until all the egg mixture has been used. Stack finished crepes as you would pancakes.

Frittata alla Carbonara

SERVINGS Makes 6 to 8 portions.

. . . .

Gluten-free, Nut-free, Refined Sugar-free, Soy-free

INGREDIENTS
- 4   bacon slices
- 8   large asparagus spears, trimmed to about 5 inches long
- 4   soft-boiled eggs

DIRECTIONS

1. Preheat oven to 425 degrees F.

2. Bring a large pot of heavily salted water to a boil. Add spaghetti and cook according to package directions. Drain the pasta, rinse with hot water and set aside.

3. Whisk eggs and cream together with 1/2 teaspoon salt and 1/2 teaspoon pepper. Whisk in Parmesan cheese.

4. Cut bacon into 1/4-inch pieces. Place in a cold, oven-proof skillet, turn heat to medium and cook until crisp, about 6 minutes. Add the drained pasta and toss to coat. Gently add the egg mixture. Bake until cooked through, 15 to 17 minutes. Loosen the sides of the frittata with a dinner knife and slide onto a cutting board or serving dish if desired.

Frittata in a Mug

SERVINGS Makes 1 portion.

Gluten-free, Grain-free, Nut-free, Refined Sugar-free, Soy-free, Vegetarian

INGREDIENTS

- 2 large eggs
- 2 tablespoons cottage cheese
- 1 small green onion, chopped
- 4 grape tomatoes, quartered
- 2 teaspoons grated Parmesan cheese
- 1 pinch kosher or fine sea salt
- 1 pinch freshly ground black pepper

DIRECTIONS

1. Grease a microwave-safe mug with vegetable oil or gluten-free, nonstick cooking spray. Add the eggs and beat lightly with a fork. Add cottage cheese, green onion, tomatoes and Parmesan cheese. Then, add salt and pepper.

2. Microwave on high for 30 seconds, stir and microwave for 45 to 60 seconds, or until the eggs are set.

Tomato Shell Egg Bake

SERVINGS Makes 1 portion.

Gluten-free, Grain-free, Nut-free, Refined Sugar-free, Soy-free, Vegetarian

INGREDIENTS
1   medium tomato
Kosher or fine sea salt, to taste
Freshly ground black pepper, to taste
1   large egg
1   tablespoon freshly grated Parmesan cheese
1   teaspoon finely minced chives

DIRECTIONS
1. Preheat oven to 350 degrees F. Grease a baking dish.

2. Cut a thin slice from the stem end of the tomato and scoop out the seeds and the pulp. Liberally sprinkle tomato with salt and pepper. Turn tomato upside down on paper towels and drain for about 10 minutes. Break the egg into the tomato shell, sprinkle with salt and pepper and bake for 20 to 25 minutes, or until egg is just set. Combine the cheese with the chives and sprinkle the mixture on top of the egg. Return to oven for 1 to 2 minutes, or until the cheese has melted.

3. Serve immediately.

FRYING THE PERFECT EGG
Heat a little oil or butter in a nonstick pan over medium-high until hot. Break an egg into the skillet and immediately reduce the heat to low. Cook the egg gently until the white is set. For a flipped egg, slide a thin spatula under the egg and gently turn it over. Cook for 1 to 2 minutes, or until the egg is cooked to your liking.

Breakfast Tostada

SERVINGS Makes 1 portion.

Gluten-free, Nut-Free, Refined Sugar-free, Soy-free, Vegetarian

INGREDIENTS

	Vegetable or olive oil, to cook
1	corn tortilla
3	tablespoons refried beans
2	tablespoons Mexican blend grated cheese
2	tablespoons prepared salsa
1	large egg
1	pinch kosher or fine sea salt
1	pinch freshly ground black pepper

DIRECTIONS

1. Position an oven rack about 6 inches from the broiler and preheat. Line a baking sheet with parchment paper.

2. Heat about 1 tablespoon of vegetable or olive oil in a small skillet until very hot. Add the tortilla and fry until golden brown and crispy on one side, about 1 minute. Flip and fry the other side for 30 seconds.

3. Pat off excess oil with a paper towel and place on the baking sheet. Spread the beans evenly over the top of the tortilla and sprinkle with cheese, broil for about 2 minutes, or until the cheese starts to melt. Top with the salsa.

4. Heat a little oil in a small skillet over medium. Fry the egg and serve on top of the tostada. Season with salt and pepper.

Flaky Biscuits

SERVINGS Makes 12 biscuits.

Gluten-free, Egg-free, Nut-free, Refined Sugar-free, Soy-free, Vegetarian, Optionally Dairy-free

INGREDIENTS

2 ¼	cups gluten-free, all-purpose flour
1	tablespoon baking powder
1	teaspoon kosher or fine sea salt
6	tablespoons cold butter or dairy-free butter sticks
¾–1	cup milk or dairy-free milk

DIRECTIONS

1. Preheat oven to 400 degrees F. Line a baking sheet with a silicone baking mat.

2. Whisk together the flour, baking powder and salt. With the large holes on a box grater, grate the butter into the flour mixture. Using your fingers, quickly work the butter into the flour, making sure to leave some large pieces.

3. Add the milk, starting with ½ a cup and gradually adding more a little bit at a time, mixing until the dough comes together. Put a little flour on a work surface and roll out the dough, kneading it a few times and patting the dough to about ¾-inch thick. Cut biscuits with a 2 ½-inch cookie cutter and gently reform dough to cut more biscuits. Place the biscuits on the prepared sheet and bake for 20 minutes, or until lightly browned. Serve warm.

Quick Blueberry Jam

SERVINGS Makes 2 cups of jam.

*Gluten-free, Grain-free, Dairy-free,
Egg-free, Nut-free, Refined Sugar-free,
Soy-free, Vegan, Vegetarian*

INGREDIENTS
- 2   pints fresh blueberries, rinsed
- ¾   cup agave nectar
- ¼   teaspoon kosher or fine sea salt
- 1   lemon, juiced

DIRECTIONS

1. Combine all ingredients in a heavy saucepan. Bring to a boil over medium-high heat. Mash berries with a potato masher or the back of a spoon. Lower the heat so mixture continues to boil gently.

2. Continue to cook uncovered for 20 to 25 minutes, or until the mixture is thick. Cool to room temperature, keeping in mind the jam will gel as it cools. Refrigerate for up to a month or freeze for up to a year.

Seriously Simple Strawberry Jam

SERVINGS Makes 1 cup of jam.

Gluten-free, Grain-free, Dairy-free, Egg-free, Nut-free, Refined Sugar-free, Soy-free, Vegan, Vegetarian

INGREDIENTS
1 pound fresh strawberries, hulled, rinsed and halved
½ cup agave nectar

DIRECTIONS
1. Combine strawberries and agave in a heavy saucepan over medium high heat and bring to a boil. Lower the heat so that the mixture continues to boil gently. Stir the mixture a few times while cooking to prevent sticking or scorching and mash the berries a few times with a potato masher or the back of a spoon.

2. Continue to cook uncovered for 25 minutes, or until berries have broken down and the mixture is very thick. Cool to room temperature, keeping in mind the jam will gel as it cools. Store in a clean jar for up to a week.

Breakfast Crostini

SERVINGS Makes 8 portions.

Gluten-free, Nut-Free, Refined Sugar-free, Soy-free, Vegetarian

INGREDIENTS

2	tablespoons olive or grape-seed oil
2	cups red seedless grapes
8	(¼-inch) diagonally sliced gluten-free baguette pieces
3	tablespoons butter, melted
2	ounces cream cheese, at room temperature
¼	cup creamy sunflower seed butter

DIRECTIONS

1. Preheat the broiler to high and place the top oven rack about 4 inches from the heat.

2. Add the oil and grapes to a medium skillet over medium heat. Cook, stirring occasionally, until the grapes are soft and just beginning to pop.

3. Brush both sides of the baguette slices with butter. Broil for 1 to 2 minutes, or until golden brown, then flip and broil the other side for 1 to 2 minutes.

4. Combine the cream cheese and sunflower seed butter. Spread mixture on the toasted bread, top with grapes and serve.

Tropical Mango and Coconut Chia Pudding

SERVINGS Makes 1 portion.

Gluten-free, Grain-free, Dairy-free, Egg-free, Refined Sugar-free, Soy-free, Vegan, Vegetarian

INGREDIENTS

- ¼ cup unsweetened coconut flakes
- ¼ cup chia seeds
- 1 cup full-fat or light coconut milk
- 1 ½ teaspoons honey
- ¼ cup diced mango (or other fruit)

DIRECTIONS

1. In a small dry skillet over medium heat, toast the coconut flakes until they're golden brown and fragrant, about 2 minutes. Reserve until time to serve.

2. Combine chia seeds, coconut milk and honey in a jar or glass. Refrigerate overnight.

3. Top pudding with toasted coconut and mango.

Crunchy Granola

SERVINGS Makes 8 (¼-cup) servings.

Gluten-free, Dairy-free, Egg-free, Refined Sugar-free, Soy-free, Vegetarian, Optionally Nut-free

INGREDIENTS

- ¼ cup creamy peanut or sunflower seed butter
- ¼ cup honey
- 2 teaspoons pure vanilla extract
- 2 cups certified gluten-free rolled oats
- ½ teaspoon kosher or fine sea salt

DIRECTIONS

1. Preheat oven to 325 degrees F. Spray a cookie sheet with gluten-free, nonstick cooking spray.

2. Combine the nut or seed butter and honey in a large, microwave-safe bowl. Microwave for 30 seconds, or until nut or seed butter has melted. Stir in vanilla, oats and salt. Make sure all the oats are coated with the mixture. Spread the mixture in an even layer on the prepared baking sheet and bake for 20 minutes, stirring once or twice while baking. Let cool. The mixture will become crunchy as it cools.

Creamy Blueberry Smoothie

SERVINGS Makes 2 adult portions or 4 child portions.

Gluten-free, Grain-free, Egg-free, Nut-free, Refined Sugar-free, Soy-free, Vegetarian

INGREDIENTS

1 ½	cups coconut water
2	cups frozen blueberries
1	cup Greek yogurt
1	large banana, peeled and cut into pieces
½	avocado, peeled and pitted
1	cup ice

DIRECTIONS

1. Combine all ingredients in a blender and blend until smooth, scraping down the sides of the container as needed.

Green Smoothie for Beginners

SERVINGS Makes 2 adult portions or 4 child portions.

Gluten-free, Grain-free, Dairy-free, Egg-free, Nut-free, Refined Sugar-free, Soy-free, Vegan, Vegetarian

INGREDIENTS

2	cups fresh spinach or kale leaves, firmly packed
2	cups water
1	cup frozen mango chunks
1	cup cantaloupe or honeydew melon chunks
1	cup frozen green grapes
½	avocado, peeled and pitted

DIRECTIONS

1. Combine all ingredients in a blender and blend until smooth, scraping down the sides of the container as needed.

Chocolate Almond Smoothie

SERVINGS Makes 1 adult portion or 2 child portions.

Gluten-free, Grain-free, Dairy-free, Egg-free, Refined Sugar-free, Soy-free, Vegan, Vegetarian

INGREDIENTS

1	cup unsweetened almond milk
4	tablespoons creamy almond butter
1 ½	tablespoons unsweetened cocoa powder
1	large banana
½	teaspoon pure vanilla extract
4-5	ice cubes

DIRECTIONS

1. Combine all ingredients in a blender and blend until smooth, scraping down the sides of the container as needed. Serve immediately.

Soups &

Light and fresh, these recipes are perfect

ROASTED
TOMATO SOUP

Salads

whether paired or eaten alone.

CHIPOTLE
BUTTERNUT
SQUASH SOUP

PRE-MADE PREP
Dressing can be prepared in advance.
Give it another whisk before adding
the rest of the salad ingredients
and toss everything together just
before serving time.

Apple, Walnut and Arugula Salad

SERVINGS Makes 4 to 6 portions.

Gluten-free, Grain-free, Dairy-free, Egg-free, Refined Sugar-free, Soy-free, Vegan, Vegetarian

INGREDIENTS

1	shallot, minced
2	tablespoons balsamic vinegar
	Kosher or fine sea salt
	Freshly ground black pepper
¼	cup olive oil
3	medium apples, cored and thinly sliced
1	cup toasted walnuts
7	ounces baby arugula

DIRECTIONS

1. In the bottom of a salad bowl, whisk together the shallot, vinegar, 1 teaspoon salt and ½ teaspoon pepper. Drizzle in the olive oil while whisking.

2. Add the apples, walnuts and arugula to the bowl and toss well. Adjust seasoning with more salt and pepper if desired.

Grilled Vegetable Salad

SERVINGS Makes 8 portions.

Gluten-free, Grain-free, Egg-free, Nut-free, Refined Sugar-free, Soy-free, Vegetarian

INGREDIENTS
- 4   red, orange or yellow bell peppers
- ¼   cup balsamic vinegar
- ½   cup olive oil
- 1   teaspoon kosher or fine sea salt
- ½   teaspoon freshly ground black pepper
- 2   medium eggplants
- 3   medium sweet onions
- 4   ounces goat cheese, crumbled

DIRECTIONS

1. Place the peppers on a grill, gas burners or under the broiler and cook, turning occasionally, until the skin is blackened all over. Place in a large mixing bowl and cover with a plate (or place in a paper bag and close it). Let peppers steam for 20 minutes. Rub the skins off the peppers. Cut them in half and remove the stems, seeds and veins. Cut into slivers about ¼-inch thick.

2. Whisk together the vinegar, oil, salt and pepper. Toss the pepper strips with 1 tablespoon of the vinegar and oil mixture.

3. Heat a grill or grill pan to medium. Slice the eggplants into ½-inch thick rounds and the onions into ¼-inch thick slices. Brush both sides of the eggplant and onion slices with the vinegar and oil mixture. Place on the grill and cook 3 minutes per side or until you have nice grill marks and the vegetables start to soften. Lightly brush the vegetables once again with the vinegar and oil mixture. Arrange the vegetables on a platter and top with the goat cheese.

Purple Potato Salad

SERVINGS Makes 6 to 8 portions

Gluten-free, Dairy-free, Nut-free, Soy-free, Vegetarian, Optionally Egg-free, Optionally Vegan

INGREDIENTS

- 3 pounds small (1 ½- to 2-inch) purple potatoes, scrubbed and halved
- 1 tablespoon plus 1 teaspoon kosher or fine sea salt, divided, plus more to taste
- 1 lime, zested and juiced
- 4 tablespoons olive oil
- ½ teaspoon freshly ground black pepper, plus more to taste
- 2 cups frozen corn kernels, thawed
- 6 green onions, white and green parts, thinly sliced
- ⅓ cup mayonnaise or vegan mayonnaise

DIRECTIONS

1. Place the potatoes in a large pot. Cover with water and add 1 tablespoon of salt. Bring to a boil, cover and cook for 10 minutes, or until fork tender. Drain.

2. Finely grate the zest of the lime into a large mixing bowl. Add the juice, olive oil, remaining 1 teaspoon salt and pepper. Whisk to combine. Add the potatoes and toss to coat. Let sit until the potatoes are cool.

3. Add the corn, green onions and mayonnaise. Gently stir to combine. Taste and add more salt and pepper if desired. Cover with plastic wrap and refrigerate for 2 to 24 hours.

Curried Rice Salad

SERVINGS Makes 6 portions.

Gluten-free, Dairy-free, Soy-Free, Vegetarian Optionally-Egg Free, Optionally Nut-free, Optionally Vegan

INGREDIENTS

1 ½	cups sliced almonds (for a nut-free version substitute chopped apples or celery for crunch)
½	cup mayonnaise or vegan mayonnaise
¼	cup mango chutney
2	tablespoons curry powder
4	cups cooked rice, cooled
	Kosher or fine sea salt, to taste
	Freshly ground black pepper, to taste

DIRECTIONS

1. Place the almonds in a large, dry skillet and cook, stirring frequently, over medium-high heat until browned and fragrant, about 5 minutes. Let cool.

2. Combine the mayonnaise, mango chutney and curry powder in a large mixing bowl and stir to combine. Add the rice and almonds and gently fold until coated with the mayonnaise mixture. Taste and season with salt and pepper, if desired. Serve immediately or cover with plastic wrap and store in the refrigerator until ready to serve.

Green Bean Salad

SERVINGS Makes 6 to 8 portions.

*Gluten-free, Grain-free,
Refined Sugar-free, Soy-free,
Vegetarian, Optionally Dairy-free*

INGREDIENTS

	Kosher or fine sea salt
1 ½	pounds thin green beans, trimmed
1	pint grape or cherry tomatoes, halved
3	tablespoons olive oil
2	tablespoons red wine vinegar
¾	teaspoon freshly ground black pepper
1	cup crumbled feta cheese
¼	cup mint leaves, chopped

DIRECTIONS

1. Fill a large bowl with ice and water.

2. Bring a pot of salted water to a boil. Add the green beans and cook for 3 minutes, or until crisp tender. Drain the beans, then immediately put them into the ice water to cool. Drain well and pat dry with paper towels.

3. Add the green beans to a mixing bowl with the tomatoes. Whisk together the olive oil, vinegar, 1 ½ teaspoons salt and ¾ teaspoon pepper. Pour over the beans and tomatoes and toss to coat.

4. Cover and refrigerate for at least 1 hour or up to 2 days. Just before serving, add the feta and mint and toss to coat.

Artichoke and Quinoa Salad

SERVINGS Makes 6 portions.

Gluten-free, Dairy-free, Egg-free, Nut-free, Refined Sugar-free, Soy-free, Vegan, Vegetarian

INGREDIENTS

6	tablespoons olive oil, divided
6	green onions, white and green parts, thinly sliced, divided
1 ½	cups pre-rinsed golden quinoa
3	cups water
1	lemon, juiced and zested
1	teaspoon kosher or fine sea salt
½	teaspoon freshly ground black pepper
1	large red pepper, seeded and diced
1	(12-ounce) jar marinated artichoke hearts, drained and coarsely chopped

DIRECTIONS

1. Heat 2 tablespoons olive oil in a large pot with a lid. Add the white and light green parts of the green onions and cook, stirring, for 2 minutes. Add the quinoa and toast for 1 minute. Add 3 cups of water and bring to a boil. Cover the pot, reduce heat to low and simmer until the water is fully absorbed and the quinoa is translucent and tender, 10 to 15 minutes. Remove from heat and let sit, covered for 5 minutes. Place the quinoa in a large mixing bowl, fluff with a fork and let cool.

2. In a small mixing bowl whisk together the remaining 4 tablespoons of olive oil, the zest and juice from the lemon (about 3 tablespoons juice), salt and pepper. Pour the mixture over the quinoa. Add the sliced dark green parts of the green onions, the bell pepper and the artichoke hearts. Stir to combine. Serve immediately or cover with plastic wrap and refrigerate until serving.

Grilled Corn Salad

SERVINGS Makes 6 portions.

Gluten-free, Dairy-free, Egg-free, Nut-free, Refined Sugar-free, Soy-free, Vegan, Vegetarian

INGREDIENTS

6 ears of corn, husks and silk removed
 Vegetable oil, to brush
 Kosher or fine sea salt
 Freshly ground black pepper
1 tablespoon balsamic vinegar
2 tablespoons olive oil
1 teaspoon herbes de provence
1 pint grape or cherry tomatoes, halved
1 cup (packed) fresh basil leaves

DIRECTIONS

1. Brush the corn with vegetable oil and season with salt and pepper. Place on a grill or grill pan over medium heat. Cook for 8 minutes, turning a quarter turn every 2 minutes. Remove from the grill and let cool.

2. In a large mixing bowl, whisk together the vinegar, olive oil, ¾ teaspoon salt, ½ teaspoon pepper and the herbes de provence.

3. Cut the corn kernels from the cobs. Add them to the dressing, along with the tomatoes, and stir to combine.

4. Stack the basil leaves on top of each other. Roll up like a cigar and cut with a very sharp knife into thin ribbons. Add the basil to the corn and tomato mixture and stir. Serve immediately or cover with plastic wrap and refrigerate.

Beet and Apple Salad

SERVINGS Makes 8 to 10 portions.

*Gluten-free, Grain-free, Dairy-free,
Egg-free, Refined Sugar-free, Soy-free,
Vegan, Vegetarian*

INGREDIENTS

8	medium beets (about 2 ½ pounds), leaves and stems cut off
½	cup olive oil
¼	cup apple cider vinegar
2	teaspoons Dijon mustard
1	teaspoon kosher or fine sea salt
½	teaspoon freshly ground black pepper
1	large Granny Smith apple, cored and thinly sliced
½	cup roasted and salted pistachios, coarsely chopped

DIRECTIONS

1. Preheat oven to 400 degrees F. Wrap each beet individually in foil. Place them on a baking sheet and roast for 1 hour, or until the beets are tender. Let cool.

2. Peel the beets and cut into thin wedges. Place in a serving bowl.

3. Whisk together the olive oil, vinegar, mustard, salt and pepper. Pour over the beets and toss to coat. Add apples and toss. (Can be made ahead up to this point and stored, covered, in the refrigerator for up to 4 hours.)

4. Before serving, add the pistachios and toss to combine.

CHEF NOTE
It is easier to peel beets after they have cooked and cooled. To keep your hands from turning red while peeling and cutting beets, wear kitchen gloves.

Summer Pasta Salad

SERVINGS Makes 8 to 10 portions.

Gluten-free, Egg-free, Refined Sugar-free, Soy-free, Vegetarian

INGREDIENTS

Kosher or fine sea salt, to taste
1 (16-ounce) box gluten-free penne or other tube-shaped pasta
1 (12-ounce) jar roasted red peppers, drained, dried and chopped
1 (16-ounce) jar prepared pesto
1 (8-ounce) ball fresh mozzarella cheese, chopped
3 cups baby arugula
Freshly ground black pepper, to taste

DIRECTIONS

1. Bring a large pot of heavily salted water to a boil and cook the pasta according to the package directions. Drain, rinse under cold water and drain again.

2. In a large mixing bowl, combine the pasta with the remaining ingredients and toss well. Season to taste with salt and pepper.

3. Serve immediately or chill, covered, in the refrigerator for up to 1 day.

Warm Potato Salad

SERVINGS Makes 8 portions.

*Gluten-free, Grain-free, Dairy-free,
Egg-free, Nut-free, Soy-free*

INGREDIENTS

2 ½   pounds (approximately 8 medium),
       Yukon Gold potatoes, cut into
       1-inch pieces
       Kosher or fine sea salt
½   pound thick-cut bacon slices
½   cup apple cider vinegar
3   tablespoons whole grain mustard
1   teaspoon sugar
       Freshly ground black pepper

DIRECTIONS

1. Place potatoes in a large pot
and cover with cold water. Add 2
teaspoons salt and bring to a boil.
Cook for 10 minutes, or until the
potatoes are tender.

2. Fry the bacon in a skillet over
medium heat until crispy, about
10 minutes. Drain the bacon on
paper towels and reserve the fat.

3. In a large mixing bowl, whisk
together the apple cider vinegar,
mustard, sugar, ½ teaspoon salt
and ½ teaspoon pepper. Whisk
in ¼ cup of the reserved bacon
fat. Add the potatoes and toss
to coat. Taste for seasoning and
add more salt and pepper, if
desired. Crumble bacon on top
and serve.

SAVE AND SERVE
This salad is best served immediately, but it can be made ahead and chilled in the refrigerator. If the salad develops a lot of liquid after chilling, transfer to a serving dish with a slotted spoon.

Watermelon Salad

SERVINGS Makes 6 to 8 portions.

Gluten-free, Grain-free, Egg-free, Nut-free, Refined Sugar-free, Soy-free, Vegetarian

INGREDIENTS

- 1 (5-pound) seedless watermelon, cut into 1-inch cubes
- 1 large (½-pound) sweet onion, diced
- ½ cup olive oil
- ¼ cup balsamic vinegar
- ¼ cup chopped fresh mint leaves, plus sprigs to garnish
- 1 teaspoon kosher or fine sea salt
- ½ teaspoon freshly ground black pepper
- 4 ounces crumbled feta cheese

DIRECTIONS

1. Combine the watermelon and onion in a mixing bowl. Whisk together the oil, vinegar, chopped mint, salt and pepper. Pour over the watermelon and onion and toss to coat. Add the crumbled feta and toss gently. Serve garnished with fresh mint sprigs if desired.

Orange and Pomegranate Salad

SERVINGS Makes 10 portions.

Gluten-free, Grain-free, Dairy-free, Egg-free, Nut-free, Refined Sugar-free, Soy-free, Vegan, Vegetarian

INGREDIENTS

- 6   medium oranges
- ¾   cup olive oil
- 3   tablespoons sherry vinegar or red wine vinegar
- 1   teaspoon kosher or fine sea salt
- ½   teaspoon freshly ground black pepper
- 10   ounces baby arugula
- 1   cup pomegranate seeds

DIRECTIONS

1. Juice one of the oranges and measure out ¼ cup of juice. Whisk the juice together with the olive oil, vinegar, salt and pepper. (Dressing can be made ahead and stored, covered, in the refrigerator until serving. Whisk before pouring over the salad.)

2. Cut a slice off the end of each remaining orange and cut off the skin and white pith. Slice the oranges into ¼-inch thick rounds, then cut each round in quarters. (Oranges can be prepared ahead and stored, covered, in the refrigerator.) Place the orange slices in a serving bowl and add the arugula and dressing. Toss to coat. Add the pomegranate seeds, toss and serve.

Grilled Romaine Salad

SERVINGS Makes 6 portions.

Gluten-free, Grain-free, Egg-free, Nut-Free, Refined Sugar-free, Soy-free, Vegetarian

INGREDIENTS

½	cup balsamic vinegar
3	heads romaine lettuce hearts, washed and dried well
1	medium (about ½ pound) white onion
	Olive oil
	Kosher or fine sea salt, to taste
	Freshly ground black pepper, to taste
4	ounces goat cheese, crumbled

DIRECTIONS

1. Pour the vinegar into a small stock pot or Dutch oven and bring to a boil. Let boil until it's reduced by half and the consistency is thick and syrupy—about 10 minutes. Remove from heat and let cool.

2. Leaving the root ends attached, cut the lettuce hearts into quarters vertically. Cut the onion in half vertically and remove the peels. Cut each onion half into 6 vertical slices. Brush the lettuce quarters with olive oil and toss the onion slices with olive oil.

3. Heat a gas or charcoal grill to medium-high. Grill the lettuce quarters about 1 to 2 minutes on each side, until they start to brown but are not too soft. Remove and transfer to a platter. Grill the onion slices until browned and soft, about 5 minutes. Scatter over the lettuce quarters.

4. Drizzle the balsamic syrup over the lettuce and onions. Drizzle with some olive oil, season with salt and pepper and top with the crumbled goat cheese.

Kale Waldorf Salad

SERVINGS Makes 8 portions.

*Gluten-free, Grain-free, Dairy-free, Egg-free,
Refined Sugar-free, Soy-free, Vegan, Vegetarian*

INGREDIENTS
- ½ cup olive oil
- ¼ cup sherry vinegar or red wine vinegar
- 1 teaspoon kosher or fine sea salt
- ¼ teaspoon freshly ground black pepper
- 6 cups chopped kale
- ½ cup raisins
- 2 medium red apples, cored and chopped
- ½ cup toasted walnut pieces

DIRECTIONS

1. Whisk together the oil, vinegar, salt and pepper. Place the kale in a serving dish with the raisins. Add the dressing and toss to coat. (Can be made ahead up to this point and stored, covered, in the refrigerator for up to 4 hours.)

2. Before serving, add the apples and walnuts and toss to combine.

Mediterranean Pasta Salad

SERVINGS Makes 6 to 8 portions.

Gluten-free, Egg-free, Refined Sugar-free, Soy-free

INGREDIENTS
- Kosher or fine sea salt
- 1 (8-ounce) box gluten-free spiral pasta
- 6 ounces sun-dried tomato pesto
- ¼ cup olive oil
- 2 cups shredded cooked chicken
- ¾ cup Kalamata olives, pitted and halved
- 8 ounces feta cheese, cut into cubes
- Freshly ground black pepper, to taste

DIRECTIONS

1. Bring a large pot of heavily salted water to a boil. Cook the pasta according to the package directions. Drain, rinse with cold water and drain again.

2. In a large mixing bowl, combine the pesto with the olive oil, whisking well. Add the pasta, chicken and olives. Stir to coat. Add the feta cheese and mix gently. Season with salt and pepper to taste and serve.

Cowboy Pasta Salad

SERVINGS Makes 8 portions.

Gluten-free, Dairy-free, Nut-free, Optionally Egg-free

INGREDIENTS

1	(16-ounce) box gluten-free penne or shell pasta
1	(16-ounce) package frozen mixed vegetables, thawed
3	cups cooked, shredded chicken
¾	cup mayonnaise or vegan mayonnaise
½	cup gluten-free barbecue sauce
	Kosher or fine sea salt, to taste
	Freshly ground black pepper, to taste

DIRECTIONS

1. Cook the pasta according to the package directions. During the last 30 seconds of cooking, toss in the thawed vegetables. Drain the pasta and vegetables. Rinse first with hot water, then cold and drain again.

2. Combine the pasta and vegetables with the chicken in a large mixing bowl. Combine the mayonnaise and barbecue sauce and add it to the pasta mixture. Stir well. Season with salt and pepper.

3. Serve immediately or refrigerate until serving.

Warm Tuscan Chicken and Bean Salad

SERVINGS Makes 6 to 8 portions.

Gluten-free, Grain-free, Dairy-free, Egg-free, Nut-Free, Refined Sugar-free, Soy-free

INGREDIENTS
- 2 tablespoons olive oil
- 4 garlic cloves, minced
- 1 tablespoon minced fresh rosemary
- 2 cups shredded cooked chicken
- 2 (15-ounce) cans white beans, drained and rinsed
- 1 teaspoon kosher or fine sea salt, plus more to taste
- ½ teaspoon freshly ground black pepper, plus more to taste
- 1 lemon, juiced and zested

DIRECTIONS

1. Heat the olive oil in a large skillet over medium. Add the garlic and rosemary and cook for 30 seconds. Add the chicken, beans, 1 teaspoon salt and ½ teaspoon pepper. Cook until heated through, about 6 minutes.

2. Add the lemon zest and lemon juice to the chicken and bean mixture and stir. Taste and adjust seasoning with more salt and pepper, if desired. Serve warm.

Cauliflower Soup

SERVINGS Makes 4 to 6 portions.

Gluten-free, Grain-free, Dairy-free, Egg-free, Nut-free, Soy-free

INGREDIENTS

- ¼ pound bacon slices
- 1 head cauliflower, cut into florets
- 4 cups gluten-free vegetable broth
- 2 garlic cloves, minced or grated
- 1 teaspoon kosher or fine sea salt
- ½ teaspoon freshly ground black pepper
- 2 tablespoons minced chives, to garnish

DIRECTIONS

1. Cut bacon into ¼-inch pieces and cook in a large skillet over medium heat until crispy, about 6 minutes. Transfer to a paper towel-lined plate and set aside.

2. Combine the cauliflower, vegetable broth, garlic, salt and pepper in a stock pot or Dutch oven and bring to a boil over high heat. Cover, reduce heat to medium-low and simmer until the cauliflower is soft, 15 to 20 minutes. Puree the soup in a blender in batches until smooth. (Make sure you remove the plastic insert from the blender top and cover the hole with a thick folded kitchen towel.) Return the soup to the pot and reheat before serving.

3. Serve garnished with reserved bacon pieces and chives.

Chipotle Butternut Squash Soup

SERVINGS Makes 4 to 6 portions.

*Gluten-free, Grain-free, Dairy-free, Egg-free,
Nut-free, Refined Sugar-free, Soy-free,
Optionally Vegan, Optionally Vegetarian*

INGREDIENTS

2	tablespoons olive oil
1	medium onion, diced
2	medium carrots, diced
1	(2 pound) butternut squash, peeled, seeded and cut into 1-inch cubes
4–5	cups gluten-free chicken or vegetable broth
1	chipotle pepper in adobo, minced, plus more sauce to garnish
	Kosher or fine sea salt, to taste
	Freshly ground black pepper, to taste

DIRECTIONS

1. In a large stock pot or Dutch oven, heat the oil over medium-high. Add the onion and carrots and sauté until soft, about 5 minutes. Add the squash, 4 cups chicken broth and chipotle pepper. Bring to a boil, cover and reduce heat to simmer until the squash is tender, about 30 minutes. Puree the soup in a blender in batches until smooth. (Make sure you remove the plastic insert from the blender top and cover the hole with a thick folded kitchen towel.)

2. If the soup is too thick, add a little more broth. Taste and season with salt and pepper. Return the soup to the pot and heat gently on the stovetop before serving. Serve with a drizzle of the adobo sauce to garnish, if desired.

Curried Pumpkin Soup

SERVINGS Makes 8 to 10 portions.

Gluten-free, Grain-free, Dairy-free, Egg-free, Nut-Free, Refined Sugar-free, Soy-free, Optionally Vegan, Optionally Vegetarian

INGREDIENTS

- 2 tablespoons red curry paste
- 4 cups gluten-free chicken or vegetable broth
- 2 (15-ounce) cans pure pumpkin puree
  Kosher or fine sea salt
  Freshly ground black pepper
- 1 (13 ½-ounce) can full-fat coconut milk
- ¼ cup roasted, salted pumpkin seeds

DIRECTIONS

1. Place the curry paste in a stock pot or Dutch oven and heat over medium until fragrant, about 1 minute. Add the chicken or vegetable broth, pumpkin puree, 1 teaspoon salt and ½ teaspoon pepper. Increase the heat to high and bring to a boil, stirring occasionally, about 7 minutes. Stir in the coconut milk and cook for 2 to 3 minutes, or until heated through. Taste and add more salt and pepper, if desired. (Can be made ahead up to this point and stored, covered, in the refrigerator. Reheat soup over medium before serving.)

2. Garnish bowls of the soup with pumpkin seeds.

Chicken Marsala Soup

SERVINGS Makes 4 portions.

*Gluten-free, Grain-free, Dairy-free,
Egg-free, Nut-free, Refined Sugar-free,
Soy-free*

INGREDIENTS

3	tablespoons olive oil
½	pound sliced mushrooms
1	teaspoon kosher or fine sea salt
½	teaspoon freshly ground black pepper
1	bunch green onions, white and green parts separated, chopped
¾	cup Marsala wine
2	cups shredded cooked chicken
4	cups gluten-free chicken stock

DIRECTIONS

1. Heat the olive oil in a stock pot or Dutch oven over medium-high. Add the mushrooms, salt and pepper. Cook until the mushrooms release their juices and start to brown, about 8 minutes. Add the white parts of the onions and cook for 1 minute. Add the wine, increase heat to high and cook until most of the wine has evaporated. Add the chicken and chicken stock.

2. Bring to a boil, then lower the heat and simmer until heated through, about 5 minutes. Garnish with the green parts of the green onions and serve immediately.

Potato Leek Soup

SERVINGS Makes 6 cups.

Gluten-free, Grain-free, Egg-free, Nut-free, Refined Sugar-free, Soy-free, Vegetarian, Optionally Dairy-free, Optionally Vegan

INGREDIENTS

2	tablespoons olive oil
4	small leeks, white parts only, cleaned and thinly sliced
1 ½	pounds golden potatoes, diced
4	cups gluten-free vegetable broth
	Kosher or fine sea salt, to taste
	Freshly ground black pepper, to taste
½	cup heavy cream (optional)

DIRECTIONS

1. In a large stock pot or Dutch oven, heat the oil over medium. Add leeks and cook until soft, about 8 minutes. Add potatoes and broth. Bring to a boil, cover and reduce to simmer until potatoes are fork-tender, about 20 minutes. Puree soup in a blender in batches until smooth. (Remove the plastic insert from the blender top and cover the hole with a thick-folded kitchen towel.) Season with salt and pepper. Return soup to the pot, add cream, reheat and serve.

Easy Black Bean Soup

SERVINGS Makes 4 portions.

Gluten-free, Grain-free, Egg-free, Nut-free, Refined Sugar-free, Soy-free, Optionally Dairy-free, Optionally Vegan, Optionally Vegetarian

INGREDIENTS

2	(15-ounce) cans black beans, drained and rinsed
2	cups gluten-free chicken or vegetable stock
½	cup prepared salsa, plus more to serve
1	teaspoon ground cumin
	Kosher or fine sea salt, to taste
	Freshly ground black pepper, to taste
¼	cup sour cream (optional)

DIRECTIONS

1. Put 1 can of black beans in a blender with the chicken or vegetable stock, ½ cup salsa and ground cumin. Blend mixture until smooth. Transfer to a stock pot or Dutch oven with the other can of beans and heat over medium. Taste and add salt and pepper, as needed.

2. Garnish with a dollop of sour cream and salsa, if desired.

Pesto Chicken Soup

SERVINGS Makes 6 portions.

Gluten-free, Grain-free, Egg-free, Refined Sugar-free, Soy-free

INGREDIENTS

6	cups gluten-free chicken stock
4	cups baby spinach
2	cups shredded cooked chicken
2	(15-ounce) cans white beans, drained and rinsed
⅓	cup basil pesto
	Kosher or fine sea salt, to taste
	Freshly ground black pepper, to taste
	Olive oil, to serve

DIRECTIONS

1. Combine the chicken stock, spinach, shredded chicken and white beans in a large stock pot or Dutch oven . Cook over medium until the soup starts to simmer. Let the mixture simmer for 5 minutes, then stir in the basil pesto. Taste and add salt and pepper, as needed. Let the soup simmer for another 2 to 3 minutes. Serve each bowl of soup with a drizzle of olive oil.

Cannellini Bean and Kale Soup

SERVINGS Makes 4 to 6 portions.

Gluten-free, Grain-free, Dairy-free, Egg-free, Nut-Free, Refined Sugar-free, Soy-free, Vegan, Vegetarian

INGREDIENTS

1	tablespoon olive oil
1	medium onion, chopped
1	(15-ounce) can fire-roasted tomatoes
4	cups gluten-free vegetable broth
1	cup water
4	cups chopped kale
2	(15-ounce) cans cannellini beans, rinsed and drained
	Kosher or fine sea salt, to taste
	Freshly ground black pepper, to taste

DIRECTIONS

1. Heat the oil in a large stock pot or Dutch oven. Add the onion and cook until softened, about 3 minutes. Add the tomatoes with any juices included in the can, the vegetable stock and water. Bring to a boil. Add the kale and simmer for 10 minutes. Add the beans and cook until heated through, about 5 minutes. Season with salt and pepper.

Roasted Tomato Soup

SERVINGS Makes 4 to 6 portions.

Gluten-free, Grain-free, Dairy-free, Egg-free, Nut-free, Refined Sugar-free, Soy-free, Vegan, Vegetarian

INGREDIENTS

1	pound plum tomatoes, quartered and seeded
3	tablespoons olive oil
½	teaspoon kosher or fine sea salt, plus more to taste
¼	teaspoon freshly ground black pepper, plus more to taste
1	large white or yellow onion, diced
3	cloves garlic, minced
1	(28-ounce) can crushed tomatoes
½	cup fresh basil leaves, plus more to garnish

DIRECTIONS

1. Preheat oven to 400 degrees F.

2. Place the plum tomatoes on a rimmed baking sheet, drizzle with 1 tablespoon olive oil and sprinkle with ½ teaspoon salt and ¼ teaspoon pepper. Roast until the tomatoes are soft and beginning to brown, 15 to 20 minutes.

3. Heat 2 tablespoons olive oil in a large stock pot or Dutch oven over medium. Add the onion and garlic and cook, stirring occasionally, until soft, about 10 minutes. Add the roasted tomatoes along with any juices and the canned tomatoes. Fill the tomato can with water and add it to the pot. Bring to a boil. Reduce the heat, add the basil and simmer uncovered for 20 minutes. Blend the soup in batches until creamy and smooth. (Remove the plastic insert from the blender top and cover the hole with a thick-folded kitchen towel.) Start the blender on low, gradually increasing the speed. Add more salt and pepper, to taste. Garnish with fresh basil leaves.

Starters &

From dips to chips to shrimp, these small

Snacks

bites are sure to hit the spot.

PICO DE GALLO

PIT TIPS
Kitchen folklore has it that placing the pit from the avocado into the guacamole will prevent it from browning.

Guacamole

SERVINGS Makes 2 cups.

Gluten-free, Grain-free, Dairy-free, Egg-free, Nut-free, Refined Sugar-free, Soy-free, Vegan, Vegetarian

INGREDIENTS

6	ripe avocados, halved and pitted
2	limes, juiced
10–12	dashes gluten-free hot sauce (more or less to taste)
1	medium red onion, finely chopped
2	Roma tomatoes, seeded and chopped
	Kosher or fine sea salt, to taste
	Freshly ground black pepper, to taste

DIRECTIONS

1. Scoop the flesh of the avocados into a mixing bowl. Mash with a fork or potato masher, leaving some larger chunks. Stir in the lime juice, hot sauce, onion and tomatoes. Season with salt and pepper.

2. Serve immediately or place the guacamole in a serving bowl and press a piece of plastic wrap directly on its surface to keep it from turning brown.

STRAIN AND SERVE
This recipe is best served within 2 hours of preparation. If you need to make it further ahead, pour pico de gallo through a strainer and discard extra liquid before serving.

DIP TIPS
This dip is best made the day before. Refrigerate for 24 hours, allowing the flavors to meld and mellow. Serve with gluten-free crackers, toasted baguette slices or crudités.

Pico de Gallo

SERVINGS Makes 2 cups.

Gluten-free, Grain-free, Dairy-free, Egg-free, Nut-free, Refined Sugar-free, Soy-free, Vegan, Vegetarian

INGREDIENTS

- 12 Roma tomatoes, seeded and chopped
- 1 large white onion, diced
- 3–4 jalapeño peppers, seeded, veined and minced
- 1 cup fresh cilantro, stems removed and chopped
- 2 limes, juiced
  Kosher or fine sea salt, to taste
  Freshly ground black pepper, to taste

DIRECTIONS

1. Combine the tomatoes, onion, jalapeños and cilantro in a large mixing bowl and stir to combine. Add the lime juice and stir. Add salt and pepper.

Giardiniera Dip

SERVINGS Makes 2 cups.

Gluten-free, Grain-free, Nut-free, Soy-free, Vegetarian, Optionally Egg-free

INGREDIENTS

- 1 (16-ounce) jar giardiniera
- 1 (8-ounce) package cream cheese, at room temperature
- 3 tablespoons mayonnaise or vegan mayonnaise
- ¼ teaspoon freshly ground black pepper
- 2 tablespoons fresh chives, minced

DIRECTIONS

1. Reserving 2 teaspoons of liquid, drain and chop giardiniera. Combine chopped giardiniera and reserved liquid with the remaining ingredients. Refrigerate until serving time.

Baked Crab Dip

SERVINGS Makes 1 ½ cups.

*Gluten-free, Grain-free, Nut-Free, Soy-free,
Optionally Dairy-free, Optionally Egg-free*

INGREDIENTS

- 1 (8-ounce) package cream cheese or dairy-free cream cheese substitute, at room temperature
- ½ cup mayonnaise or vegan mayonnaise
- 1 ½ teaspoons gluten-free seafood seasoning (such as Old Bay)
- 1 lemon, juiced
- 1 (16-ounce) can crabmeat, rinsed and drained
  Kosher or fine sea salt, to taste
  Freshly ground black pepper, to taste

DIRECTIONS

1. Preheat oven to 400 degrees F. In a mixing bowl, combine the crea m cheese and mayonnaise until smooth. Add the seafood seasoning and lemon juice and stir well. Fold in the crabmeat. Season with salt and pepper. If preparing the dip the day before, cover with plastic wrap and refrigerate.

2. Transfer to an oven-safe baking dish and bake until the dip is hot and browned, about 15 minutes. Serve warm with endive leaves, vegetables or gluten-free crackers.

BLT Deviled Egg Dip

SERVINGS Makes 2 cups.

*Gluten-free, Grain-free, Dairy-free,
Nut-free, Soy-free*

INGREDIENTS

3	slices gluten-free bacon, diced
12	hard-boiled eggs, peeled and halved
½	cup mayonnaise
1	tablespoon yellow mustard
3	medium plum tomatoes, seeded and finely chopped
	Kosher or fine sea salt, to taste
	Freshly ground black pepper, to taste

DIRECTIONS

1. Place bacon in a cold frying pan. Cook over medium heat, stirring occasionally, until crispy. Drain on paper towels.

2. Scoop the yolks into a mixing bowl and smash with a fork until fairly smooth. Add the mayonnaise and mustard and mash to combine. Finely chop the egg whites and add them to the yolk mixture. Reserve a little of the bacon and tomatoes and stir the rest into the dip. Season with salt and pepper. Refrigerate until ready to serve. Garnish with the reserved bacon and tomato before serving. Serve with gluten-free crackers or lettuce leaves.

White Bean Dip

SERVINGS Makes 2 cups.

Gluten-free, Grain-free, Dairy-free,
Egg-free, Nut-free, Refined Sugar-free,
Soy-free, Vegan, Vegetarian

INGREDIENTS

- 2 (15-ounce) cans of cannellini beans, drained and rinsed
- 3 cloves garlic, grated or minced
- ⅓ cup plus 1 tablespoon olive oil, divided
- 2 teaspoons ground cumin
- 1 teaspoon kosher or fine sea salt
- ½ teaspoon freshly ground black pepper

DIRECTIONS

1. Place the beans, garlic, ⅓ cup olive oil, cumin, salt and pepper in the bowl of a food processor. Process until smooth. Serve immediately topped with remaining oil or store in the refrigerator covered with plastic wrap for up to three days.

Pea and Mint Crostini

SERVINGS Makes 12 to 14 portions.

Gluten-free, Egg-free, Nut-free, Refined Sugar-free, Soy-free, Vegetarian

INGREDIENTS

- 1 gluten-free baguette
- ¼ cup plus 6 tablespoons olive oil, divided
- 1 (10-ounce) bag frozen peas, thawed
- ½ cup grated Parmesan cheese
- ½ cup (packed) fresh mint leaves, plus more to garnish
- ½ teaspoon kosher or fine sea salt
- ½ teaspoon freshly ground black pepper

DIRECTIONS

1. Preheat oven to 375 degrees F. Line a baking sheet with parchment paper or a silicone baking mat.

2. To make the crostini, cut the baguette into ½-inch slices, place the slices on the prepared baking sheet and brush the tops with ¼ cup olive oil. Bake for 7 to 8 minutes, or until golden brown. Let cool.

3. Place the remaining 6 tablespoons olive oil, peas, Parmesan cheese, mint leaves, salt and pepper in a food processor and process with long pulses until all the ingredients are combined but the mixture is still a bit chunky. Spread the pea mixture on the crostini. Garnish with mint leaves, if desired, and serve.

Cranberry Orange Baked Brie

SERVINGS Makes 6 portions.

Gluten-free, Grain-free, Egg-free, Soy-free, Vegetarian

INGREDIENTS
- 1 (8- to 9-ounce) round Brie cheese
- ½ cup whole cranberry sauce
- ¼ cup gluten-free orange sauce
- ¼ cup roasted, salted pistachios, chopped

DIRECTIONS

1. Preheat oven to 350 degrees F. Line a baking sheet with parchment paper or a silicone baking mat. Place Brie on the sheet and bake for 5 to 7 minutes, or until softened.

2. In a small saucepan, combine the cranberry and orange sauces. Bring to a boil over medium heat and let cook for 2 to 3 minutes, or until thickened. Place the Brie on a serving dish, top with the orange-cranberry sauce and chopped pistachios. Serve with gluten-free crackers.

Chili Lime Roasted Chickpeas

SERVINGS Makes 10 to 12 portions.

Gluten-free, Grain-free, Dairy-free, Egg-free, Nut-free, Refined Sugar-free, Soy-free, Vegan, Vegetarian

INGREDIENTS

- 2 (15-ounce) cans chickpeas (garbanzo beans), rinsed and drained
- 2 tablespoons olive oil
- 2 tablespoons chili powder
- ½ teaspoon dried cumin
- 1 lime, juiced
  Kosher or fine sea salt, to taste

DIRECTIONS

1. Transfer drained chickpeas to a double layer of paper towels and rub with another paper towel to dry. Let sit for 30 minutes.

2. Preheat oven to 400 degrees F. Line 2 baking sheets with parchment paper or a silicone baking mat. Spread the beans in a single layer on the prepared baking sheet. Bake for 45 minutes, shaking the pan occasionally. Do not turn the oven off.

3. In a medium mixing bowl, combine the olive oil with the chili powder, cumin and lime juice. Add the beans to the mixture and toss well to coat.

4. Return the beans to the baking sheet and bake for another 10 to 15 minutes, or until the beans are crisp but not burned. Sprinkle with salt. Transfer to a serving bowl and serve chickpeas warm or at room temperature.

Salt and Vinegar Kale Chips

SERVINGS Makes 8 portions.

Gluten-free, Grain-free, Dairy-free, Egg-free, Nut-free, Refined Sugar-free, Soy-free, Vegan, Vegetarian

INGREDIENTS
- 1 bunch kale, washed and dried well
- 1 tablespoon olive oil
- 1½ teaspoons apple cider vinegar
  Kosher or fine sea salt, to taste

DIRECTIONS
1. Preheat oven to 300 degrees F. Line 2 baking sheets with parchment paper or silicone baking mats.

2. Remove and discard the stem from each leaf of kale. Tear the leaves into large bite-sized pieces. Toss in a large bowl with oil and vinegar. Lay kale on prepared baking sheets in a single layer. Sprinkle with salt.

3. Bake for 20 minutes, or until crisp. Let the chips cool, then serve.

Maple Ginger Pecans

SERVINGS Makes 8 portions.

*Gluten-free, Grain-free, Egg-free,
Refined Sugar-free, Soy-free, Vegetarian,
Optionally Vegan*

INGREDIENTS

¼   cup unsalted butter or dairy-free
      butter substitute
⅓   cup maple syrup
1   (2- by 1-inch) piece of fresh ginger,
      peeled and minced or grated
1   teaspoon kosher or fine sea salt
¼–½ teaspoon gluten-free hot sauce
4   cups pecan halves

DIRECTIONS

1. Preheat oven to 300 degrees F.
Line a baking sheet with
parchment paper or a silicone
baking mat. In a small saucepan
over medium heat, combine the
butter, maple syrup, ginger, salt
and hot sauce. Bring to a boil, then
reduce heat to low and simmer for
2 minutes.

2. Place nuts in a mixing bowl,
add the maple glaze and stir well
to coat. Pour onto the prepared
baking sheet and spread into an
even layer.

3. Bake for 30 to 40 minutes,
or until dry, stirring every
10 minutes. Let cool.

Potato Latkes

SERVINGS Makes 20 to 24 latkes.

Gluten-free, Grain-free, Nut-free, Refined Sugar-free, Soy-free, Vegetarian, Optionally Dairy-free

INGREDIENTS

- 2 pounds (about 6 medium) russet potatoes
- 1 medium onion, peeled
- 1 large egg
- 1 teaspoon kosher or fine sea salt, plus more to taste
- ½ teaspoon freshly ground black pepper
- ¾ cup vegetable oil, divided
- Sour cream or applesauce, to serve

DIRECTIONS

1. Preheat oven to 200 degrees F. Line a baking sheet with paper towels. Grate potatoes with the large holes of a box grater. Soak potatoes in a large bowl of ice water for 1 to 2 minutes. Place in a kitchen towel and squeeze out all liquid. Place potatoes in a mixing bowl. Grate onion into potatoes. Add egg, salt and pepper. Stir well to combine.

2. Heat ¼ cup oil in a large skillet over medium. Once oil is hot, drop 2 tablespoons of potato mixture per latke into oil. Cook for 5 minutes, or until golden brown, then flip. Cook for another 5 minutes, or until crispy. Remove latkes from pan and place on paper towel-lined baking sheet. Sprinkle with salt and keep warm in oven while frying remaining latkes. Continue until all latkes are fried. Add more oil as needed between batches, letting it heat fully before adding potato mixture.

3. Serve latkes with sour cream, applesauce or both.

Barbecue Meatballs

SERVINGS Makes 36 meatballs.

Gluten-free, Egg-free, Nut-free, Soy-free, Optionally Dairy-free

INGREDIENTS

4	slices gluten-free bread, crusts removed and bread torn into small pieces
½	cup milk or dairy-free milk
2	pounds ground chuck
½	medium white or yellow onion
1	teaspoon kosher or fine sea salt
½	teaspoon freshly ground black pepper
1	(18-ounce) bottle gluten-free barbecue sauce

DIRECTIONS

1. Preheat oven to 375 degrees. Place the torn bread into a large mixing bowl and pour the milk over it. Let mixture sit for 5 to 10 minutes.

2. Add the ground chuck. Using the large holes of a box grater, grate the onion into the bowl. Add the salt and pepper. Mix to combine well.

3. Shape the mixture into 1-inch balls and place them on a rimmed baking sheet or in a 9- by 13-inch baking dish. If making the meatballs ahead of time, cover and refrigerate them until ready to serve. Bake for 25 minutes. Leave the oven on.

4. Drain any grease from the baking pan. Pour the barbecue sauce over the meatballs and gently toss to coat. Return the meatballs to the oven for another 10 minutes, or until cooked through. Serve warm. Leftover meatballs can be reheated at 350 degrees F for about 10 minutes.

Chicken-Apple Skewers

SERVINGS Makes 6 to 8 skewers.

Gluten-free, Dairy-free, Egg-free, Nut-free

INGREDIENTS

½ pound boneless, skinless chicken breasts, cut into 1 ½-inch cubes
½ teaspoon kosher or fine sea salt
¼ teaspoon freshly ground black pepper
2 tablespoons gluten-free Asian barbecue sauce, plus more to serve, if desired
2 large apples, cored and cut into 1 ½-inch chunks
1 lemon, juiced

DIRECTIONS

1. Preheat oven to 400 degrees F. Line a baking sheet with foil. Place the chicken cubes in a small mixing bowl, add the salt, pepper and barbecue sauce. Toss to coat.

2. Place the chicken in a single layer on the prepared baking sheet and bake for 15 minutes, or until the chicken is no longer pink inside. Let cool.

3. Toss the apples with lemon juice. Once the chicken has cooled, thread onto small skewers, alternating with apple chunks. If preparing the night before, wrap the skewers in plastic wrap and refrigerate. Serve with more barbecue sauce on the side, if desired.

Sticky Wings

SERVINGS Makes 8 portions.

Gluten-free, Dairy-free, Egg-free, Nut-free, Refined Sugar-free

INGREDIENTS

½ cup gluten-free teriyaki sauce
½ cup honey
3 pounds chicken wing drummettes
2 teaspoons toasted sesame seeds

DIRECTIONS

1. Preheat oven to 475 degrees F. Line 2 rimmed baking sheets with foil.

2. Combine teriyaki sauce with honey. Pour ½ mixture into a large mixing bowl, add chicken wings and toss to coat.

3. Place the chicken wings on the prepared baking sheets, skin side down and bake for 20 minutes. Discard leftover marinade.

4. Remove 2 tablespoons from remaining teriyaki and honey mixture. Pour remaining sauce into a small serving bowl.

5. Flip chicken wings, brush with 2 tablespoons sauce and cook for another 2 minutes.

6. Sprinkle wings with sesame seeds and serve with reserved sauce.

Crispy Chicken Wings

SERVINGS Makes 4 to 6 portions.

Gluten-free, Dairy-free, Egg-free, Nut-free, Soy-free

INGREDIENTS
- 1   cup gluten-free barbecue sauce, divided
- ½   cup honey, divided
- 4   pounds chicken wing drumettes
- 1   (9-ounce) box gluten-free crackers

DIRECTIONS

1. Pour ¾ cup of barbecue sauce and ¼ cup of honey in a large plastic food storage bag and mix to combine. Add the chicken wings, close the bag and toss several times to coat the wings with sauce. Refrigerate for at least 30 minutes or up to 24 hours.

2. Preheat oven to 450 degrees F. Spray 2 baking sheets with gluten-free, nonstick cooking spray.

3. Grind crackers in a food processor or blender until fine crumbs form. Pour the crumbs onto a dinner plate. Remove a chicken wing from the marinade, roll it in cracker crumbs and place it on one of the prepared baking sheets. Repeat with the remaining chicken wings. Discard leftover marinade.

4. Lightly spray the tops of the wings with gluten-free, nonstick cooking spray. Bake for 25 to 30 minutes, or until the wings are brown, cooked through and an instant-read thermometer inserted into the thickest part of the wing registers 165 degrees F.

5. Combine the remaining ¼ cup of barbecue sauce with the remaining ¼ cup of honey and serve the mixture with wings.

Prosciutto-Wrapped Shrimp

SERVINGS Makes 6 portions.

Gluten-free, Grain-free, Dairy-free, Egg-free, Nut-free, Refined Sugar-free, Soy-free

INGREDIENTS

24	(6-inch) wooden skewers
3	tablespoons olive oil, divided
1	lemon, juiced, divided
	Kosher or fine sea salt
	Freshly ground black pepper
24	large shrimp, peeled and deveined
8	thin slices prosciutto
4	cups baby arugula

DIRECTIONS

1. Soak the skewers in water for 30 minutes. Combine 2 tablespoons of olive oil, half the lemon juice, a generous pinch of salt and a generous pinch of pepper in a large plastic food storage bag. Add the shrimp and marinate for 10 minutes. Pat the shrimp dry and discard the marinade.

2. Cut each of the prosciutto slices in thirds lengthwise. Wrap 1 prosciutto strip around each shrimp. Push a skewer through the shrimp from the tail to the head.

3. Heat a grill or grill pan to medium. Cook the shrimp for about 3 minutes per side, or until the prosciutto starts to brown and the shrimp are cooked through.

4. Toss the arugula with 1 tablespoon of olive oil and the remaining lemon juice. Season to taste with salt and pepper and transfer to a serving platter. Arrange the shrimp on top of the arugula and serve.

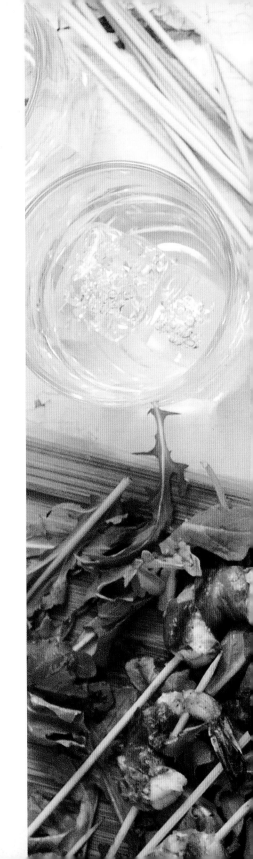

Roasted Shrimp with Wasabi Cocktail Sauce

SERVINGS Makes 4 to 6 portions.

Gluten-free, Dairy-free, Nut-free, Refined Sugar-free, Soy-free

ROASTED SHRIMP

INGREDIENTS

2	pounds shrimp, peeled, cleaned and deveined, tails left on
1	teaspoon kosher or fine sea salt
1	teaspoon freshly ground black pepper
4	teaspoons Old Bay Seasoning
1	tablespoon olive oil
1	lemon, juiced

DIRECTIONS

1. Preheat oven to 400 degrees F.

2. Place shrimp on a baking sheet. Season with salt, pepper, Old Bay, olive oil and lemon juice. Toss to coat and spread shrimp out in an even layer. Roast for 5 to 6 minutes.

3. Serve with Wasabi Cocktail Sauce.

WASABI COCKTAIL SAUCE

INGREDIENTS

1	cup mayonnaise
2	tablespoons prepared wasabi (more or less to taste)
1	lime, finely zested and juiced, plus more to garnish

DIRECTIONS

1. Mix mayonnaise with wasabi, lime zest and lime juice until well blended. Garnish with lime wedges, if desired, and serve with shrimp.

Grilled Clams

SERVINGS Makes 6 portions.

Gluten-free, Grain-free, Egg-free, Nut-free, Refined Sugar-free, Soy-free

INGREDIENTS
5	whole lemons
½	cup unsalted butter, at room temperature
4	garlic cloves, minced
1	green onion, minced
1 ½	pounds littleneck clams, scrubbed

DIRECTIONS

1. Cut 4 lemons into wedges and reserve them for serving.

2. Finely grate the zest of the remaining lemon and juice it. Combine the butter, garlic and green onion with the lemon juice and zest.

3. Heat a grill to medium. Place the clams directly on the grill, cover and cook for 6 to 8 minutes, or until clams open.

4. Transfer the clams to a serving platter, dot with the butter mixture and serve with lemon wedges.

Gazpacho Shooters

SERVINGS Makes 12 shots.

Gluten-free, Grain-free, Dairy-free, Egg-free, Nut-free, Refined Sugar-free, Soy-free, Vegan, Vegetarian

INGREDIENTS

2 ½   cups tomato juice, cold, divided
1   garlic clove, minced
1   jalapeño pepper, seeded, veined and finely chopped
1   seedless cucumber, peeled and finely chopped
1   yellow or orange bell pepper, seeded and finely chopped

DIRECTIONS

1. In a blender, puree 1 cup of the tomato juice with the garlic and jalapeño. Pour the mixture into a bowl, add the rest of the tomato juice and stir in the cucumber and bell pepper pieces.

2. Refrigerate mixture until ready to serve. Pour into 2-ounce shot glasses and enjoy.

Pimento Cheese Deviled Eggs

SERVINGS Makes 12 deviled eggs.

Gluten-free, Grain-free, Nut-free, Soy-free, Vegetarian

INGREDIENTS

6   hard-boiled eggs, peeled and halved
¼   cup mayonnaise
2   tablespoons jarred pimentos, chopped
⅓   cup grated sharp cheddar cheese
2–3   dashes gluten-free hot sauce
   Kosher or fine sea salt, to taste
   Freshly ground black pepper, to taste

DIRECTIONS

1. Scoop the egg yolks into a mixing bowl and smash with a fork until fairly smooth. Add the mayonnaise, pimentos, cheese and hot sauce. Mash everything together until smooth and season with salt and pepper. Pipe or spoon the yolk mixture into the egg whites.

2. Refrigerate until ready to serve.

STORE AND SERVE
Dates can be made a day ahead and stored, covered with plastic wrap, in the refrigerator. Reheat in the microwave for 45 seconds to 1 minute before serving.

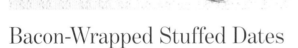

Bacon-Wrapped Stuffed Dates

SERVINGS Makes 24 dates.

Gluten-free, Grain-free, Egg-free, Nut-free, Refined Sugar-free, Soy-free

INGREDIENTS
24	Medjool dates
4	ounces goat cheese, softened
12	slices gluten-free bacon

DIRECTIONS

1. Preheat oven to 400 degrees F. Place a wire cooling rack on a rimmed baking sheet. Cut a lengthwise slit into each date, remove the pit and stuff with goat cheese. Pinch the dates closed.

2. Cut the bacon slices in half crosswise. Wrap each date securely with the bacon and place seam side down on the wire rack. Bake for 10 minutes, flip dates over and bake for another 10 minutes, or until the bacon is crispy. Serve warm or at room temperature.

Baked Jalapeño Poppers

SERVINGS Makes 40 poppers.

Gluten-free, Grain-free, Nut-free, Refined Sugar-free, Soy-free, Vegetarian

INGREDIENTS
20	large jalapeño peppers
1	(8-ounce) package cream cheese, at room temperature
2	cups grated sharp cheddar cheese, at room temperature
¼	cup mayonnaise

DIRECTIONS

1. Preheat oven to 425 degrees F. Line 2 baking sheets with parchment paper or silicone baking mats. Cut the peppers in half lengthwise and scrape out the seeds and veins. Combine the cheeses and mayonnaise and mix well. Spread the cheese mixture into the peppers and bake for 15 minutes, or until the cheese starts to brown. Serve warm.

Easy En

PISTACHIO
MINT CRUSTED
LAMB

trees

These mains are all you need to make for an easy evening of entertaining.

Easy Beef Brisket

SERVINGS Makes 6 portions.

Gluten-free, Grain-free, Dairy-free, Egg-free, Nut-free, Soy-free

INGREDIENTS

1	teaspoon kosher or fine sea salt
½	teaspoon freshly ground black pepper
1	(3-pound) beef brisket, fat trimmed
1	large white or yellow onion, thinly sliced
1	(12-ounce) bottle gluten-free barbecue sauce
1 ½	cups water
1	(10-ounce) can regular or spicy gluten-free diced tomatoes with green chilies
1 ½	pounds small white potatoes, scrubbed and unpeeled

DIRECTIONS

1. Preheat oven to 325 degrees F.

2. Combine the salt and pepper in a small bowl and rub the mixture over the brisket. Transfer the brisket to a baking dish. Cover the beef with the sliced onions.

3. Combine the barbecue sauce, water and canned tomatoes with chilies. Pour the mixture over the beef and cover the dish with foil. Bake for 3 hours. Leave the oven on.

4. Remove the foil, add the potatoes and cook, uncovered, for another 40 to 45 minutes, or until the potatoes are tender. Let rest for 10 minutes, slice the beef and return to the dish. Spoon the sauce over the beef and serve.

Pork Chops au Poivre

SERVINGS Makes 4 portions.

Gluten-free, Egg-free, Nut-free, Refined Sugar-free, Soy-free

INGREDIENTS

1	teaspoon kosher or fine sea salt
1	tablespoon freshly ground black pepper
4	(4-ounce) boneless center-cut pork chops
1	tablespoon olive oil
3	tablespoons butter, divided
2	medium shallots, minced
½	cup brandy
½	cup heavy cream

DIRECTIONS

1. Combine salt and pepper. Pat the mixture well on both sides of the pork chops.

2. Heat the oil and 1 tablespoon butter in a large skillet over medium-high. Add the chops and cook until browned on both sides and cooked through, 2 to 3 minutes per side. Remove the chops from the skillet, transfer them to a plate and cover with foil.

3. Pour out the fat from the skillet, return to the stove over medium heat and add the remaining 2 tablespoons butter. Cook the shallots for 3 minutes. Add the brandy and cook until most of the liquid has evaporated. Add the cream and cook, stirring until the sauce is hot. Serve the chops with the sauce poured over top.

Oven-Roasted Maple Mustard Salmon

SERVINGS Makes 4 portions

Gluten-free, Nut-free, Refined Sugar-free, Soy-free, Optionally Dairy-free

INGREDIENTS

- 3 tablespoons Dijon or whole grain mustard
- 1 tablespoon maple syrup
- 4 (4-ounce) skin-on salmon fillets
  Kosher or fine sea salt, to taste
  Freshly ground black pepper, to taste
- ¼ cup gluten-free panko-style bread crumbs
- ¼ cup melted butter or dairy-free butter substitute

DIRECTIONS

1. Preheat the oven to 400 degrees F. Line a baking sheet with foil.

2. Combine the mustard and maple syrup in a small bowl. Season the salmon generously on both sides with salt and pepper. Place the salmon on the prepared baking sheet, skin-side down. Brush with the mustard mixture. Top with bread crumbs and drizzle with melted butter.

3. Bake for 15 minutes and serve.

Mussels in Garlic Wine Sauce

SERVINGS Makes 4 portions.

Gluten-free, Grain-free, Dairy-free, Egg-free, Nut-free, Refined Sugar-free, Soy-free

INGREDIENTS

- 2 tablespoons olive oil
- 8 garlic cloves, minced
- 2 lemons, zested and juiced
- 4 cups dry white wine
- 4 pounds mussels, scrubbed and debearded
- 2 cups fresh Italian parsley, chopped
  Kosher or fine sea salt, to taste
  Freshly ground black pepper, to taste

DIRECTIONS

1. Heat the oil in a large stock pot over medium. Add the garlic and cook for 30 seconds. Add the lemon zest, juice and wine. Bring to a boil.

2. Add the mussels and cover the pot. Boil, stirring occasionally, for 4 to 5 minutes, or until the shells have opened. Discard any mussels that did not open. Stir in the parsley. Season with salt and pepper and serve.

CUPCAKES FOR DINNER
Top meat loaves with mashed
potatoes and tell the kids they are
having cupcakes for dinner. They will
come running to the table!

Mini Meat Loaves

SERVINGS Makes 6 portions.

Gluten-free, Dairy-free, Nut-free, Soy-free

INGREDIENTS

1	tablespoon olive oil
2	slices soft gluten-free bread or 1 cup gluten-free bread crumbs
1 ¼	pounds lean ground turkey or beef
1	large egg
⅓	cup plus ¾ cup gluten-free barbecue sauce, divided
1	teaspoon kosher or fine sea salt
½	teaspoon freshly ground black pepper
1	medium yellow onion, peeled

DIRECTIONS

1. Preheat oven to 450 degrees F. Brush 12 cups of a standard muffin pan with olive oil.

2. Place the bread in a blender and pulse until it turns to crumbs. (Omit this step if you are using already prepared breadcrumbs.) Pour the crumbs into a large mixing bowl. Add the turkey or beef, egg, ⅓ cup barbecue sauce, salt and pepper. With the large holes of a box grater, grate the onion into the mixture, then mix to combine. Do not over mix. Place about ⅓ cup of the meat mixture into each prepared muffin tin and gently press down to fill. Top each with 1 tablespoon of barbecue sauce.

3. Bake for 20 minutes, or until the meat loaves are cooked through. Run a dinner knife around the edges of the muffin tins, remove the meat loaves from the pan and serve.

Wild Mushroom Risotto

SERVINGS Makes 6 portions.

Gluten-free, Egg-free, Nut-free, Refined Sugar-free, Soy-free, Optionally Dairy-free, Optionally Vegan, Optionally Vegetarian

INGREDIENTS
- 3   tablespoons olive oil, divided
- 1 ½   pounds assorted wild mushrooms, cut into pieces
    Kosher or fine sea salt, to taste
    Freshly ground black pepper, to taste
- 2   bunches green onions, white and green parts, sliced, divided
- 1 ½   cups Arborio rice
- 6   cups gluten-free chicken or vegetable broth, heated
- ½   cup Parmesan cheese or dairy-free Parmesan substitute

DIRECTIONS
1. Heat 1 tablespoon of oil in a large skillet or Dutch oven over medium-high. Add the mushrooms and cook, stirring occasionally, until browned, about 10 minutes. Season with salt and pepper. Remove the mushrooms from the skillet and set aside.

2. Heat the remaining 2 tablespoons of oil over medium-high. Add the white parts of the green onions and cook for 2 to 3 minutes. Add the rice and cook, stirring for 3 to 4 minutes, or until the rice is transparent. Add about 1 cup of warm broth and stir frequently until most of the broth is absorbed. Continue adding warm broth in the same manner, cooking and stirring until the liquid is absorbed, all of the broth is used and the rice is tender and creamy. Stir in the reserved mushrooms and Parmesan cheese.

3. Stir in the green portion of the onions and serve.

SIMPLE SUBS
If you prefer—and dairy isn't an issue—
use half milk and half water in place
of rice milk. For spicier sauce,
you can also use 1 can of mild chilies
and 1 can of spicy chilies.

Shrimp and Grits

SERVINGS Makes 6 portions.

*Gluten-free, Dairy-free, Egg-free, Nut-free, Soy-free,
Refined Sugar-free*

INGREDIENTS

4	cups unflavored, unsweetened rice milk
1 ½	teaspoons kosher or fine sea salt, divided, plus more to taste
1 ⅓	cups gluten-free grits
2	tablespoon olive oil, divided, plus more if desired
1	bunch green onions, white and green parts, chopped
2	(10-ounce) cans gluten-free diced tomatoes with green chilies
¼	teaspoon freshly ground black pepper, plus more to taste
1 ½	pounds medium shrimp, peeled and deveined, tails on or off

DIRECTIONS

1. Bring the rice milk and 1 teaspoon of salt to a boil in a large saucepan. Gradually stir in the grits. Lower the heat and simmer, stirring frequently, until the mixture is thick and creamy, about 20 minutes (or according to the package directions). For extra richness, stir in 1 tablespoon of olive oil once the grits are done.

2. Heat 1 tablespoon of olive oil in a large skillet over medium-high. Add the white parts of the green onions. Sauté for 1 minute. Add both cans of diced tomatoes with green chilies along with the juice, ½ teaspoon salt and ¼ teaspoon pepper. Cook, uncovered, until the liquid has evaporated, about 6 minutes. Add the shrimp and cook, uncovered, for 5 minutes, or until the shrimp is pink and opaque. Remove from the heat and stir in the green parts of the green onions. Taste and add more salt and pepper, if desired.

3. Serve the shrimp mixture over the grits.

Shrimp Scampi

SERVINGS Makes 6 portions.

*Gluten-free, Grain-free, Egg-free,
Nut-free, Refined Sugar-free, Soy-free,
Optionally Dairy-free*

INGREDIENTS

- 4 tablespoons butter or dairy-free butter substitute
- 3 garlic cloves, minced
- ¼ cup dry vermouth or white wine
- 1 ½ pounds uncooked shrimp, peeled and deveined
     Kosher or fine sea salt, to taste
     Freshly ground black pepper, to taste
- 2 tablespoons minced fresh parsley

DIRECTIONS

1. In a large skillet over medium heat, melt the butter. Add the garlic and cook for 30 seconds. Add the vermouth or wine and cook for 1 to 2 minutes, or until the liquid is mostly evaporated. Add the shrimp and cook, stirring occasionally, until pink and opaque, 3 to 4 minutes. Season with salt and pepper. Stir in the parsley.

2. Serve shrimp over rice or gluten-free pasta, if desired.

BUTTERFLIED CHOPS

To butterfly a pork chop, first set the meat flat on a cutting board and place your hand gently over the meat. Hold a sharp knife parallel to the cutting board and slice horizontally through the meat, slowly moving the knife back and forth. Do not cut all the way through the meat—stop when you are a bit more than ⅔ through. Gently pull the meat open like a book.

Pear and Cranberry-Stuffed Pork Chops

SERVINGS Makes 4 portions.

Gluten-free, Grain-free, Dairy-free, Nut-free, Soy-free

INGREDIENTS

- 4 thick-cut boneless pork chops
- 1 bunch green onions, white and green parts
- 1 teaspoon gluten-free poultry seasoning
- 1 ½ teaspoons kosher or fine sea salt
- ½ teaspoon freshly ground black pepper
- 1 tablespoon olive oil, plus more to brush
- 2 firm but ripe pears, peeled, cored and cut into ¼-inch dice
- ½ cup dried cranberries

DIRECTIONS

1. Preheat oven to 350 degrees F.

2. Butterfly the pork chops and pat dry with paper towels. Slice the white and light green parts of the green onions and mince the green tops. Combine the poultry seasoning with the salt and pepper.

3. In a large, oven-safe skillet, heat 1 tablespoon olive oil over medium-high. Add the white and light green parts of the green onions and sauté for 1 minute. Add the pears, cranberries and 1 teaspoon of the poultry seasoning mixture and cook, stirring often, until the pears are tender and starting to brown, about 8 minutes. Transfer the mixture to a bowl and wash and dry the skillet.

4. Sprinkle half the remaining poultry seasoning mixture on the insides of the pork chops. Rub it in well. Spoon heaping tablespoons of the pear mixture into the center of each pork chop. Close and secure the openings with toothpicks. You will have a little more than half the pear mixture left over. Reserve this for later. Brush both sides of the pork chops with some olive oil and season with the remaining poultry seasoning mixture.

5. Heat the skillet over medium-high. Add the pork chops and sear for 2 to 3 minutes. Flip and sear the other side for 1 to 2 minutes. Place the skillet in the oven and cook for 20 to 25 minutes, or until an instant-read thermometer inserted into the meat reads 160 degrees F. Transfer the pork chops to a serving platter. Put the skillet (along with any juices that have accumulated during cooking) on the stove over medium-high heat. Add the reserved pear mixture and cook for 1 minute, stirring to coat the mixture with the pan juices. Take off the heat and stir in the minced green onion tops. Remove the toothpicks from the chops, spoon the pear mixture on top and serve.

tenderizer until the steak is even in thickness and about ¼-inch thick. Alternatively, you can ask your butcher to run the steak through their meat tenderizer and then pound it with a rolling pin. Season the meat with salt and pepper. Spread half the cheese in a 3-inch wide strip down the center of the meat.

2. Drain and finely chop the sun-dried tomatoes and place on top of the cheese. Top with about 1 ½ cups spinach leaves and sprinkle lightly with some salt and pepper. Roll the steak up tightly, starting at one edge of the long side, tucking in the filling as you go. Brush the meat on the outside with olive oil and season well with salt and pepper. Place the steak on a cutting board and score the meat into 8 even-sized pieces about 1 ½ inches thick. Tie the meat between the score marks in 8 places with butcher twine and cut the meat at the score marks.

3. Brush a baking sheet with olive oil. Place the pinwheels on the baking sheet and bake for 25 minutes, or until the meat is cooked to your liking. Let rest a few minutes, then remove the strings.

4. About 10 minutes before the meat is done, place the pine nuts in a large dry skillet over medium-high heat and toast until brown and fragrant, about 3 to 4 minutes. Remove the pine nuts and reserve. Add 1 tablespoon of olive oil to the hot pan and add the remaining spinach. Sauté until the spinach is wilted, 3 to 4 minutes.

5. Place the remaining cheese in a blender or small food processor with 2 tablespoons of olive oil and a large pinch of salt and pepper. Process until smooth and pourable. If the sauce is too thick, add a few more drops of olive oil.

6. For each serving, place 2 pinwheels on a bed of sautéed spinach with a drizzle of the sauce and a sprinkling of pine nuts.

Stuffed Flank Steak Pinwheels with Sautéed Spinach

SERVINGS Makes 4 portions.

Gluten-free, Grain-free, Nut-free, Soy-free, Refined Sugar-free

INGREDIENTS

1 ¼	pounds flank steak
	Kosher or fine sea salt, to taste
	Freshly ground black pepper, to taste
1	(5.2-ounce) container garlic and herb cheese spread
⅔	cup sun-dried tomatoes in olive oil
2	(6-ounce) bags prewashed baby spinach
⅓	cup pine nuts
3	tablespoons olive oil, divided, plus more to brush

DIRECTIONS

1. Place the flank steak between 2 pieces of plastic wrap. Pound with the pronged side of a meat

Pork Roast with Cider Gravy

SERVINGS Makes 4 to 6 portions.

Gluten-free, Dairy-free, Egg-free, Nut-free, Soy-free

INGREDIENTS

2	tablespoons olive oil
1	(2 ½-pound) pork roast, trimmed and tied
	Kosher or fine sea salt, to taste
	Freshly ground black pepper, to taste
1	medium white or yellow onion, peeled and sliced
1	medium apple, cored and sliced
1	medium pear, cored and sliced
1	(12-ounce) bottle gluten-free hard apple cider

DIRECTIONS

1. Preheat oven to 375 degrees F.

2. In a Dutch oven or oven-safe covered pan, heat the oil over medium. Season the pork on all sides generously with salt and pepper and brown, about 4 minutes per side. Remove the pork from the pan and set aside.

3. Add the onion, apple and pear to the pan. Season with a large pinch of salt and pepper. Cook until soft and beginning to brown, about 8 minutes. Add the cider, scraping the pan to release any of the brown bits at the bottom of the pan. Add the pork back into the pan. Cover and bake in the oven until the pork registers 145 degrees F on an instant-read thermometer, about 40 minutes.

4. Remove the pork from the pan, place it on a cutting board and tent it with foil. Let the pork sit for 10 minutes.

5. Puree the cider mixture in a blender. Pour back into the pan and bring to a boil. Season with salt and pepper.

6. Slice the pork and serve with gravy on the side.

Pork & Sweet Potato Skewers

SERVINGS Makes 6 portions.

Gluten-free, Grain-free, Dairy-free, Egg-free, Nut-free, Refined Sugar-free, Soy-free

INGREDIENTS

1	large (¾-pound) sweet potato
1	(1- to 1 ¼-pound) pork tenderloin
2	green apples
4	tablespoons olive oil
1	teaspoon kosher or fine sea salt
½	teaspoon freshly ground black pepper
¼	cup honey, to serve
¼	cup gluten-free Dijon or stone ground mustard, to serve

DIRECTIONS

1. Soak 12 (6-inch) or 6 (12-inch) wooden skewers in water for at least 10 minutes. Preheat oven to 350 degrees F.

2. Peel the sweet potato and cut it into 12 slices. Cut each slice in half. Place the sweet potato slices in a medium skillet and cover with cold water. Bring to a boil and let cook, uncovered, for 5 minutes, or until just tender. Rinse with cold water and dry with paper towels.

3. Cut the pork into 24 (1-inch) slices. Core the apples and cut each one into 12 slices.

4. Combine the olive oil with the salt and pepper. Alternate the pork, sweet potatoes and apples on the skewers (2 pieces of each on the small skewers, 4 on the large). Place the skewers in a single layer on 2 baking sheets and brush with the olive oil mixture.

5. Bake for 8 minutes, turn the skewers over and bake for another 8 minutes, or until the pork is cooked through.

6. Combine the honey and mustard and serve with the skewers to dip.

SERVING TIP
Serve Provencal Fish en Pappillotte in
parchment on dinner plates and
let each diner cut open their packet.
The immediate release of fragrant
steam is part of the experience.

Provencal Fish en Pappillote

SERVINGS Makes 6 portions.

Gluten-free, Grain Free, Dairy-free, Egg-free, Nut-free, Soy-free, Refined Sugar-free

INGREDIENTS
- 1 large fennel bulb
- 4 (4- to 6-ounce) fillets cod, haddock or other firm white fish, about ¾-inch thick
  Kosher or fine sea salt, to taste
  Freshly ground black pepper, to taste
- 2 medium tomatoes, seeded and chopped
- ¼ cup pitted kalamata olives, chopped
- 1 lemon, zested and juiced

DIRECTIONS

1. Preheat oven to 400 degrees F. Cut 4 (15- by 30-inch) pieces of parchment paper and fold in half to make a square. Cut out a half heart shape (like when making paper Valentines) and open.

2. Slice the fennel thinly, reserving some of the fronds. Lay a quarter of the fennel close to the center line on one half of each piece of parchment. Pat the fish fillets dry with a paper towel and sprinkle lightly with some salt and pepper on both sides. Lay the fish over the fennel. Top with tomatoes, olives, salt and pepper. Top the fillets with lemon zest, lemon juice and a few sprigs of reserved fennel fronds.

3. Fold the other half of the parchment over the ingredients. Make small overlapping folds to seal the edges, starting at the top of the heart. When you have about two inches of parchment left, twist the remaining paper twice to seal. Place the packets on a baking sheet and bake for 15 minutes.

Grilled Fish Tacos

SERVINGS Makes 6 portions.

Gluten-free, Dairy-free, Nut-free, Soy-free, Optionally Egg-free

INGREDIENTS

6	(4- to 6-ounce) tilapia fillets
	Olive oil, as needed
	Kosher or fine sea salt, to taste
	Freshly ground black pepper, to taste
3	cups finely shredded cabbage
1	tablespoon gluten-free mango salsa, plus more to serve
2	tablespoons mayonnaise or egg-free mayonnaise
12	gluten-free corn tortillas

DIRECTIONS

1. Brush the tilapia fillets with olive oil and season with salt and pepper. Heat a large skillet over medium high. Place the tilapia fillets in the skillet and cook without disturbing for 2 minutes. Flip and cook for another 2 minutes, or until the fish is cooked through and just starts to flake. Remove the fillets from the skillet, break into large flakes and keep warm.

2. Mix the cabbage with mango salsa and mayonnaise.

3. Heat the tortillas. Serve the tortillas with some of the cabbage mixture and the shredded fish fillets. Top with additional salsa.

Black Bean Tostadas

SERVINGS Makes 6 portions.

Gluten-free, Egg-free, Nut-free,
Refined Sugar-free, Soy-free, Vegetarian,
Optionally Dairy-free, Optionally Vegan

INGREDIENTS

	Grape-seed or vegetable oil, to fry
12	gluten-free corn tortillas
1	recipe Refried Black Beans without cheese (page 188)
½	head iceberg lettuce, thinly sliced
	Kosher or fine sea salt, to taste
	Freshly ground black pepper, to taste
¼	recipe Pico de Gallo (page 86)
8	ounces queso fresco or Monterey Jack cheese, crumbled or grated (optional)

DIRECTIONS

1. Preheat oven to 250 degrees F. Line a baking sheet with paper towels.

2. Pour enough oil in a large skillet to reach ¼-inch. Heat over medium until the oil sizzles but does not smoke. Add one tortilla at a time and fry individually until golden brown, about 30 seconds each. (The oil should sizzle immediately. If it does not, the oil is not hot enough.) Flip and fry the other side of each tortilla until golden brown. Remove to the paper towel-lined baking sheet and keep warm in the oven until all the tortillas are fried.

3. Heat the refried black beans. Season the shredded lettuce with salt and pepper.

4. To serve, layer the fried tortillas with the refried black beans, lettuce, Pico de Gallo and cheese.

Butternut Squash and Watercress Pasta

SERVINGS Makes 6 portions.

Gluten-free, Dairy-free, Egg-free, Soy-free, Refined Sugar-free, Vegan, Vegetarian, Optionally Nut-free

INGREDIENTS

2 ½	pounds butternut squash, peeled, seeded and cut into ¾-inch cubes
1	tablespoon olive oil, plus more to drizzle
½	teaspoon kosher or fine sea salt, plus more to boil and taste
¼	teaspoon freshly ground black pepper, plus more to taste
½	cup chopped walnuts (omit for nut-free)
1	(12-ounce) box brown rice gluten-free penne pasta
2	cups watercress, thick stems removed

DIRECTIONS

1. Preheat oven to 450 degrees F. Place the butternut squash on a baking sheet and toss to coat with 1 tablespoon olive oil, salt and pepper.

Roast for 20 minutes or until the squash is soft and starting to brown, flipping the squash one or two times while roasting for even browning.

2. Place the walnuts, if using, in a dry skillet and toast over medium heat until brown and fragrant, about 4 to 5 minutes. Set aside.

3. Bring a large pot of heavily salted water to a boil. Add the pasta and cook according to package directions. Reserve about 1 cup of cooking water. Drain pasta and rinse with hot water.

4. Return the pasta to the pot. Add the roasted butternut squash, ¼ cup of the reserved pasta water and the watercress. Stir to combine. Add more pasta water if needed. Taste and adjust seasoning with more salt and pepper, if desired. Serve the pasta with an extra drizzle of olive oil and a sprinkling of chopped walnuts, if using.

Vegetable Curry

SERVINGS Makes 6 portions.

----

*Gluten-free, Grain-free, Dairy-free,
Egg-free, Nut-Free, Refined Sugar-free,
Soy-free, Vegan, Vegetarian*

INGREDIENTS

- 2 tablespoons olive oil
- 1 large yellow onion, halved and thinly sliced
- 3 large sweet potatoes, peeled and cut into 1-inch cubes
- 2-4 tablespoons gluten-free red curry paste
- 1 (14-ounce) can coconut milk
- 1 (14-ounce) can garbanzo beans, rinsed and drained

DIRECTIONS

1. Heat the oil in a large skillet over medium-high. Add the onion and sweet potatoes and cook until the vegetables are just starting to brown, 4 to 5 minutes. Add the curry paste to taste and stir to combine. Stir in the coconut milk. Cover, lower the heat and simmer until the vegetables are tender, 10 to 15 minutes. Remove the lid from the pan, add the garbanzo beans and cook for 1 to 2 minutes, or until heated through.

2. Serve with rice, if desired.

Chicken Teriyaki

SERVINGS Makes 6 portions.

Gluten-free, Dairy-free, Egg-free, Nut-free

INGREDIENTS

- 1 ½ pounds boneless, skinless chicken breasts, cut into 1-inch cubes
- ⅓ cup gluten-free teriyaki sauce
- 2 tablespoons vegetable or grape-seed oil
- 4 cups broccoli florets
- 2 red bell peppers, seeded and cut into thin strips
- 1 (8-ounce) can sliced water chestnuts, drained

DIRECTIONS

1. Toss the chicken with the teriyaki sauce and let marinate for 10 minutes.

2. Heat oil in a large skillet over high until it starts to shimmer. Add the broccoli and red pepper strips and cook for 2 minutes, stirring. Add the water chestnuts and cook for 1 minute, stirring. Remove the vegetables from the pan and reserve.

3. Add the chicken and teriyaki sauce to the pan. Cook, stirring for about 4 minutes, or until the chicken is cooked through. Add the vegetables back to the pan and cook for 1 minute more.

4. Serve with rice, if desired.

Spaghetti alla Carbonara

SERVINGS Makes 4 portions.

Gluten-free, Nut-free, Refined Sugar-free, Soy-free

INGREDIENTS

- Kosher or fine sea salt, to taste
- 1 (16-ounce) box gluten-free spaghetti
- ⅓ pound thick-sliced bacon, diced
- 5 large eggs yolks
- ¼ cup heavy cream
- 1 cup grated Parmesan cheese
- Freshly ground black pepper, to taste

DIRECTIONS

1. Bring a large pot of heavily salted water to a boil. Add the spaghetti and cook the pasta according to the package directions.

2. While the pasta is cooking, fry the bacon in a large skillet over medium heat until the bacon is crisp. Leave the bacon and grease in the skillet. If the pasta is not yet ready, remove skillet from heat.

3. Whisk the egg yolks with the cream and half the cheese. When the spaghetti is cooked al dente, remove 2 to 3 tablespoons of the starchy pasta cooking water and whisk it into the egg yolk mixture. Drain the pasta. Add to the skillet with the bacon, turn the heat back to medium and toss the pasta with the bacon and grease for 1 minute. Take the skillet off the heat, add the egg mixture and stir quickly to coat. Season with salt and lots of pepper. Top with the remaining cheese and serve immediately.

Chicken Parmesan Pasta

SERVINGS Makes 4 portions

Gluten-free, Egg-free, Nut-free, Refined Sugar-free, Soy-free

INGREDIENTS

- ½ teaspoon kosher or fine sea salt, plus more to boil
- 3 cups gluten-free fusilli or penne
- 1 gluten-free rotisserie chicken
- 1 tablespoon minced fresh rosemary
- 1 cup grated Parmesan cheese, divided
- ½ teaspoon freshly ground black pepper
  Olive oil, to serve

DIRECTIONS

1. Bring a large pot of heavily salted water to a boil, add the pasta and cook according to the package directions. Reserve 1 cup of cooking water, drain the pasta and return it to the pot.

2. While the pasta is cooking, shred the chicken, discarding the skin and bones. Add the chicken to the drained pasta with the reserved cooking water, rosemary, ¾ cup of Parmesan cheese, ½ teaspoon salt and ½ teaspoon pepper. Cook, stirring, over medium-low heat until the sauce thickens slightly, 3 to 4 minutes.

3. Drizzle with olive oil, sprinkle with remaining ¼ cup Parmesan cheese and serve.

Kielbasa and Kale Fettuccini

SERVINGS Makes 4 portions.

Gluten-free, Egg-free, Nut-free, Refined Sugar-free, Soy-free, Optionally Dairy-free

INGREDIENTS

  Kosher or fine sea salt, to taste
- ¾ pound kale, tough leaves and ribs removed, coarsely chopped
- 1 pound gluten-free fettuccini
- 1 tablespoon olive oil, plus more to serve
- 1 pound gluten-free turkey kielbasa, cut into ¼-inch slices
- 1 cup gluten-free chicken broth
- ½ cup grated Parmesan cheese, plus more to serve (omit for dairy-free)
  Freshly ground black pepper, to taste

DIRECTIONS

1. Bring a large pot of heavily salted water to a boil. Add kale and blanch, 5 minutes. Remove with a sieve and drain. Return water to a boil, add fettuccini and cook according to package directions. Reserve 1 cup cooking water, drain pasta and reserve.

2. Heat oil in a 12-inch skillet over medium-high. Add kielbasa and brown, 3 to 4 minutes per side. Add kale and cook, stirring, until tender, 5 minutes. Add broth, fettuccini and ½ cup cooking water. Stir in cheese and more cooking water, if needed. Add salt, pepper, oil and Parmesan as desired and serve.

Roasted Vegetable Rigatoni

SERVINGS Makes 4 portions.

Gluten-free, Egg-free, Nut-free, Refined Sugar-free,
Soy-free, Vegetarian

INGREDIENTS

  3   cups broccoli florets
  1   small red onion, halved and sliced into ¼-inch half-moons
  2   tablespoons olive oil
  ½   teaspoon kosher or fine sea salt, plus more to boil
      and taste
  ½   teaspoon freshly ground black pepper, plus more
      to taste
  ½   pound gluten-free rigatoni
  ½   cup grated Parmesan cheese

DIRECTIONS

1. Preheat oven to 400 degrees F. Place broccoli and
onion on a rimmed baking sheet. Sprinkle with oil,
salt and pepper. Roast, turning once, for 20 minutes,
or until the vegetables are tender.

2. Bring a large pot of heavily salted water to a boil.
Add the rigatoni and cook according to package
directions. Reserve 1 cup of cooking water, drain
the pasta and return to the pot. Add ½ cup of the
pasta water and the roasted vegetables. Cook for 1
minute, stirring. Add more water if the pasta seems
dry. Season to taste with salt and pepper, if needed.
Sprinkle Parmesan cheese on top and serve.

Spaghetti with Eggplant & Peppers

SERVINGS Makes 4 to 6 portions.

Gluten-free, Dairy-free, Egg-free, Nut-free,
Refined Sugar-free, Soy-free, Vegan, Vegetarian

INGREDIENTS

  1   medium eggplant, peeled and cut into 1-inch pieces
  2   red peppers, seeded, stemmed and cut into 1-inch pieces
  2   tablespoons olive oil, plus more to drizzle
  1   teaspoon kosher or fine sea salt
  ½   teaspoon freshly ground black pepper
  1   whole head of garlic, top cut off to expose cloves
  1   (16-ounce) box gluten-free spaghetti
  1   (14-ounce) can fire roasted tomatoes

DIRECTIONS

1. Preheat oven to 400 degrees F. Put eggplant and
peppers on a rimmed baking sheet. Top with oil,
salt and pepper and toss. Top garlic with oil, salt and
pepper, wrap in foil and add to baking sheet. Roast
40 to 45 minutes, stirring once or twice.

2. Bring pot of heavily salted water to a boil. Add
spaghetti and cook by package directions. Reserve
½ cup cooking water and drain pasta. Heat tomatoes
in a skillet over medium-high. Squeeze in garlic
and stir. Add eggplant and peppers. Boil and add
cooking water. Cook until sauce slightly reduces, 3 to
4 minutes. Turn off heat, add pasta and toss to coat.
Add salt and pepper, drizzle with olive oil and serve.

Garlic Roasted Chicken with New Potatoes

SERVINGS Makes 4 to 6 portions.

Gluten-free, Grain-free, Dairy-free, Egg-free, Nut-free, Refined Sugar-free, Soy-free

INGREDIENTS
3	small garlic heads, peeled and separated into cloves
7	tablespoons olive oil, divided
	Kosher or fine sea salt, to taste
	Freshly ground black pepper, to taste
1	whole chicken, butterflied
1 ½	pounds baby Yukon Gold or other new potatoes (about 1-inch in size)
1	cup baby arugula, minced
2	tablespoons fresh lemon juice

DIRECTIONS

1. Preheat the oven to 350 degrees F.

2. Place the garlic in a roasting pan or on a rimmed sheet pan. Drizzle with 1 tablespoon olive oil, salt and pepper. Rub 1 tablespoon olive oil all over the chicken and season well with salt and pepper. Place the chicken on top of the garlic, making sure all the cloves are under the chicken. Roast for 45 minutes.

3. In a mixing bowl, toss the potatoes with 1 tablespoon of the olive oil and season with salt and pepper.

4. Remove the pan from the oven. Move the garlic from under the chicken, add the potatoes to the pan and distribute garlic evenly among potatoes. Roast for another 45 minutes, or until the potatoes are tender and the chicken is golden brown.

5. While the chicken is roasting, whisk together the arugula, lemon juice, remaining olive oil, salt and pepper. Serve chicken drizzled with the arugula dressing.

Garlic Shrimp and Artichoke Heart Quinoa

SERVINGS Makes 4 to 6 portions.

Gluten-free, Dairy-free, Egg-free, Nut-free, Refined Sugar-free, Soy-free

INGREDIENTS

1 ½	cups water
½	teaspoon kosher or fine sea salt, plus more to boil and taste
1	cup pre-rinsed quinoa
6	tablespoons olive oil, divided
1	(14-ounce) can baby artichoke hearts in water
3	garlic cloves, thinly sliced
1	pound medium shrimp, peeled and deveined, tails on or off
2	tablespoons fresh lemon juice
¼	teaspoon freshly ground black pepper, plus more to taste

DIRECTIONS

1. Bring water to a boil. Add 1 teaspoon of salt and quinoa. Return to a boil, cover the pot and reduce heat to a simmer. Cook for 15 minutes, or until all the liquid is absorbed. Remove from the heat and let sit for 5 minutes. Fluff with a fork.

2. Drain the artichoke hearts, pat dry with paper towels and cut in half lengthwise. Heat a large skillet over medium-high. Add 1 tablespoon olive oil and let heat for a few seconds. Add the cut artichoke hearts and cook for 5 to 6 minutes, or until starting to brown, stirring gently occasionally. Add the sliced garlic and cook for 30 seconds.
Add 1 more tablespoon of the oil to the pan. Let heat for a few seconds and then add the shrimp. Cook, stirring gently occasionally, for 3 to 4 minutes or until the shrimp turn pink, starts to curl and is opaque, not translucent. Add to the cooked quinoa.

3. Combine the remaining 4 tablespoons of olive oil with the lemon juice, salt and pepper. Pour over the shrimp and quinoa and toss to coat. Season with additional salt and pepper, if desired.

Snapper and Asparagus with Chili Oil and Avocado Cream

SERVINGS Makes 4 portions.

Gluten-free, Grain-free, Dairy-free, Egg-free, Nut-free, Refined Sugar-free, Soy-free

INGREDIENTS

2	red Fresno chilies, seeded, deveined and finely chopped
4	tablespoons fresh lime juice, divided
4	tablespoons olive oil, divided
2	ripe avocados, halved and pitted
1	pinch kosher or fine sea salt, plus more to taste
1	pinch freshly ground black pepper, plus more to taste
1	pound asparagus
4	(8-ounce) snapper fillets or other lean white fish fillets, skin on

DIRECTIONS

1. Combine the chilies with 3 tablespoons of lime juice and 2 tablespoons of olive oil. Set aside.

2. Scoop the center of the avocados into a bowl. Add the remaining 1 tablespoon lime juice and a big pinch of salt and pepper. Mash until smooth and set aside.

3. Cut the woody ends off the asparagus spears. Working with one asparagus spear at a time, place it flat on a work surface and peel the skin off the bottom half of the stalk with a vegetable peeler. Season the peeled asparagus and fish fillets with salt and pepper and brush with the remaining oil.

4. Heat a large skillet over high. Cook the asparagus for 2 to 4 minutes, or until crisp tender. Remove from the skillet and set aside. Place the fish, skin side down, in the skillet and cook for 4 minutes. Flip and cook for another 1 to 2 minutes, or until cooked through.

5. Divide the asparagus between 4 plates. Top with the fish fillets, drizzle with the chili oil and serve with a dollop of avocado cream on the side.

Spaghetti with Pea Pesto

SERVINGS Makes 4 to 6 portions.

Gluten-free, Egg-free, Refined Sugar-free, Soy-free, Vegetarian

INGREDIENTS

½   teaspoon kosher or fine sea salt, plus more to boil
1   (1-pound) package gluten-free spaghetti
⅓   cup plus 1 tablespoon olive oil, divided
1   (10-ounce) package frozen peas
2   large cloves garlic
½   cup pine nuts
½   cup grated Parmesan cheese, plus more to serve
½   teaspoon freshly ground black pepper

DIRECTIONS

1. Bring a large pot of heavily salted water to a boil. Add the spaghetti and cook according to the package directions. Reserve about 1 cup of cooking water. Drain the spaghetti, transfer it back into the hot pot and drizzle with 1 tablespoon of olive oil. Toss gently to coat the pasta with the oil.

2. While the spaghetti is cooking, make the pesto: Bring a pot of salted water to a boil. Add the peas and cook for 2 to 3 minutes, or until cooked through. Drain well. Reserve a small handful of the peas to garnish.

3. Place the garlic in a food processor and chop finely. Add the cooked peas, pine nuts, Parmesan cheese, salt and pepper. Process until everything is finely chopped. With the motor running, drizzle in the remaining ⅓ cup olive oil and process until smooth and fully combined.

4. Add the pesto to the spaghetti along with some of the starchy pasta water. Stir to coat, adding more water a little at a time to thin the sauce if needed. Garnish with the reserved peas and more Parmesan cheese, if desired.

DON'T FORGET

It's important to remove the membrane from your ribs before you proceed to the next steps. Otherwise, the flavors won't meld properly, and the membrane can get caught in your teeth.

Fall-off-the-Bone Baby Back Ribs

SERVINGS Makes 4 to 6 portions.

Gluten-free, Grain-free, Dairy-free, Egg-free, Nut-free, Soy-free

INGREDIENTS
- 5 pounds baby back ribs
- 1 (2-liter) bottle cola (not diet)
- Kosher or fine sea salt, to taste
- Freshly ground black pepper, to taste
- ½ cup gluten-free barbecue sauce

DIRECTIONS

1. Flip the ribs bone side up and insert a dinner knife just under the white membrane that covers the meat and bones. Gently peel the membrane off and discard. Place the ribs in a baking dish or roasting pan and pour the cola over them. Cover with plastic wrap and refrigerate overnight.

2. Preheat oven to 275 degrees F. Remove the ribs from the cola and discard the cola. Pat the ribs dry with paper towels and season liberally with salt and pepper on both sides. Clean the baking dish and place the ribs back in it. Cover with foil and bake for 3 hours to 3 hours 30 minutes, or until the meat is very tender.

3. When the ribs finish baking in the oven, remove them, turn the broiler on high and position the top rack 8 inches from the broiler. Place ribs on a baking sheet, bone side down and brush with the barbecue sauce. Broil for 3 to 5 minutes, watching to make sure the sauce does not burn.

Pistachio Mint Crusted Lamb

SERVINGS Makes 6 portions.

Gluten-free, Grain-free, Dairy-free, Egg-free, Refined Sugar-free, Soy-free

INGREDIENTS

2	racks of lamb (6–8 bones each), trimmed and frenched
	Kosher or fine sea salt, to taste
	Freshly ground black pepper, to taste
3	tablespoons olive oil, divided
½	cup pistachios, shelled, roasted and salted
3	cups fresh mint leaves, loosely packed
3	garlic cloves, minced
1	lemon, zested and juiced

DIRECTIONS

1. Preheat oven to 450 degrees F.

2. Heat an oven-safe skillet or roasting pan large enough to hold both racks of lamb over medium-high. Season the lamb generously with salt and pepper on all sides. Add 1 tablespoon of the olive oil to the hot pan and sear the lamb on all sides for about 2 minutes per side. Let cool slightly.

3. Put the pistachios in a food processor and pulse a few times to grind them. Add the remaining 2 tablespoons of olive oil and the mint, garlic, lemon zest and lemon juice. Process until it turns into a paste. Spread the paste on the meat side of the lamb, pressing down firmly. Place the racks back into the skillet or pan, bone side down, and roast for 20 minutes for medium rare or 25 minutes for medium. Remove the lamb from oven. Cover loosely with foil. Let rest for 10 minutes before cutting the lamb into chops using a thin, sharp knife.

Kung Pao Pork

SERVINGS Makes 4 portions.

Gluten-free, Dairy-free, Egg-free

INGREDIENTS

- ¼ cup plus 1 tablespoon roasted peanuts, divided
- 2 tablespoons vegetable oil
- 1 pound pork tenderloin, fat trimmed and cut into 1-inch cubes
- 8 Thai chilies
- 3 green onions, cleaned, trimmed and sliced, divided
- ¼ cup gluten-free Szechuan sauce

DIRECTIONS

1. Roughly chop 1 tablespoon of the peanuts and set aside to garnish.

2. Heat the oil in a large skillet or wok over high until it begins to shimmer. Add the pork and cook for 4 minutes, turning frequently to brown on all sides. Add the remaining ¼ cup peanuts, chilies and about ⅔ of the green onions. Cook for 30 seconds, stirring constantly. Add the Szechuan sauce and cook for 1 minute, stirring constantly. Serve immediately topped with the chopped peanuts and remaining green onions.

Turkey Teriyaki in Lettuce Cups

SERVINGS Makes 8 cups.

Gluten-free, Dairy-free, Egg-free, Nut-free

INGREDIENTS

1	pound lean ground turkey
1	tablespoon vegetable oil
1	(12-ounce) bag stir fry vegetables (or a combination of shredded carrots and snow peas)
½	cup gluten-free teriyaki sauce, plus more to serve
¾	cup bean sprouts
8	iceberg, butter or romaine lettuce leaf cups

DIRECTIONS

1. Heat a large skillet or wok over high. Add the turkey and cook, breaking the turkey up with a spatula until browned and no longer pink, about 4 minutes. Remove the turkey from the pan.

2. Heat the oil in the skillet, then add the stir fry vegetables. Cook for 1 minute, stirring. Add the turkey back to the pan, along with ½ cup teriyaki sauce. Cook, stirring, for 1 minute. Stir in the bean sprouts and remove the skillet from heat.

3. Spoon the stir fry mixture into the lettuce cups and serve with more teriyaki sauce on the side.

Chicken and Broccoli Stir-Fry

SERVINGS Makes 4 portions.

Gluten-free, Dairy-free, Egg-free, Nut-free

INGREDIENTS

1	pound boneless, skinless chicken breasts
⅓	cup gluten-free teriyaki sauce
2	tablespoons vegetable oil
3	cups broccoli florets, large pieces cut in half
1 ½	cups matchstick sliced carrots
1	(8-ounce) can sliced water chestnuts, drained

DIRECTIONS

1. Cut the chicken into 1-inch pieces. Place in a bowl with the teriyaki sauce, stir to coat and marinate for 10 minutes.

2. Heat the oil in a large skillet or wok until it starts to shimmer. Add the broccoli and carrots and cook, stirring, for 2 minutes. Add the drained water chestnuts and cook, stirring, for 1 minute. Remove the vegetables from the pan and reserve.

3. Lower the heat to medium and add the chicken and teriyaki sauce mixture to the pan. Cook, stirring often, until the chicken is cooked through, about 4 minutes. Add the vegetables back to the pan with the chicken and cook for 1 minute. Serve immediately.

Chicken Fettuccine Alfredo

SERVINGS Makes 6 portions.

----

*Gluten-free, Egg-free, Nut-free,
Refined Sugar-free, Soy-free*

INGREDIENTS

	Kosher or fine sea salt, to taste
1	(16-ounce) box gluten-free fettuccine
4	tablespoons unsalted butter
2	cups heavy cream
2	cups shredded cooked chicken
1 ¼	cups grated Parmesan cheese, plus more to serve
	Freshly ground black pepper, to taste

DIRECTIONS

1. Bring a pot of salted water to a boil. Cook the fettuccine according to package directions. Reserve 2 cups of the cooking water, drain the pasta and rinse with hot water.

2. Heat the butter in a large skillet over medium. Add the cream and ½ cup of the pasta water. Bring to a simmer. Add the fettuccine, chicken and 1 ¼ cups Parmesan cheese. Toss to coat. Season with salt and pepper. If the pasta is dry, add more of the pasta cooking water, a little at a time. Serve immediately with additional Parmesan sprinkled on top.

Baked Scotch Eggs

SERVINGS Makes 6 portions.

*Gluten-free, Dairy-free, Nut-Free,
Refined Sugar-free, Soy-free*

INGREDIENTS

2	raw eggs
1 ½	pounds gluten-free country sausage
6	hard-boiled eggs, peeled
1	cup gluten-free panko-style bread crumbs
1	teaspoon kosher or fine sea salt
½	teaspoon freshly ground black pepper
	Grape-seed or vegetable oil, to brush

DIRECTIONS

1. Preheat oven to 400 degrees F.
Line a baking sheet with parchment
paper or a silicone baking mat.

2. Place the raw eggs in a bowl and
beat lightly.

3. Divide the sausage into 6 equal
portions and shape into thin patties.
Shape the sausage patties around the
hard-boiled eggs.

4. Place the bread crumbs in a shallow
bowl or on a plate, add the salt and
pepper and mix. Roll the sausage-
covered eggs first in the beaten egg
mixture, then in the bread crumbs,
pressing lightly so the crumbs adhere.
Place on the prepared baking sheet.
Brush the eggs with oil and bake for
30 minutes, or until golden brown.

Cornmeal-Crusted Chicken Nuggets

SERVINGS Makes 4 to 6 portions.

Gluten-free, Dairy-free, Nut-free, Refined Sugar-free, Soy-free, Optionally Egg-free

INGREDIENTS

1 ½	pounds chicken tenders, cut in half
1	teaspoon kosher or fine sea salt
½	teaspoon freshly ground black pepper
⅓	cup gluten-free cornmeal
1 ½	tablespoons vegetable oil
2	tablespoons Dijon or whole grain mustard
2	tablespoons mayonnaise or vegan mayonnaise

DIRECTIONS

1. Sprinkle chicken tenders with salt and pepper. Place cornmeal in a bowl, add the seasoned chicken and toss well to coat. Discard any leftover cornmeal.

2. Heat oil in a large skillet over medium. Add the chicken and cook, turning once or twice, until browned and cooked through, 6 to 8 minutes.

3. Combine the mustard and mayonnaise and serve the sauce with the chicken nuggets to dip.

Grilled Orange Chicken Skewers

SERVINGS Makes 4 skewers.

Gluten-free, Grain-free, Dairy-free, Egg-free, Nut-free

INGREDIENTS
- 6   boneless, skinless chicken thighs
- ½   cup gluten-free Asian orange sauce
- ½   cup honey
- 2   teaspoons sesame seeds

DIRECTIONS
1. Cut chicken into 1 ½-inch pieces. Combine the orange sauce and honey and put half in a medium mixing bowl; reserve the rest for later. Add the chicken pieces to the bowl and toss to combine. Let the chicken marinate for 20 minutes at room temperature or for up to 4 hours in the refrigerator. If you are marinating in the refrigerator, let it come to room temperature for 20 minutes before grilling. If using wooden skewers, soak 4 skewers in water for 20 minutes.

2. Preheat the grill to moderately high heat (450 degrees F on a gas grill).

3. Divide the chicken pieces onto 4 skewers, allowing them to touch, but making sure the pieces do not cram together. Brush the grates of the grill with oil.

4. Grill for 4 minutes with the lid closed. Turn skewers over and grill another 4 minutes, covered. Brush the reserved orange-honey sauce onto the chicken and cook for another 2 minutes, turning several times, or until the chicken is cooked through but still juicy. Sprinkle with sesame seeds and serve.

Polynesian Kebabs

SERVINGS Makes 8 skewers.

Gluten-free, Grain-free, Dairy-free, Egg-free, Nut-free

INGREDIENTS
2 ½	pounds extra-lean pork tenderloin
1	cup gluten-free Polynesian sauce, divided
1	large fresh pineapple, peeled and cored
2	green peppers
1	large red onion

DIRECTIONS

1. Cut pork into 24 pieces, roughly 1 ½-inch squares. Place in a medium mixing bowl with ½ cup Polynesian sauce and toss to combine. Let sit for 20 to 30 minutes at room temperature or up to 4 hours refrigerated. (If marinating in the refrigerator, let come to room temperature for 20 minutes before grilling.) If using wooden skewers, soak them in water for 20 minutes. Preheat the grill to moderately high heat (450 degrees F on a gas grill).

2. Cut the pineapple into 2-inch chunks. Cut the peppers in half, remove the seeds and cut them into 2-inch chunks. Cut the onion into quarters.

3. Remove the pork from the Polynesian sauce. Thread the skewers with the pork and vegetables starting and ending with pork (3 pieces of pork per skewer).

4. Brush the grates of the grill with oil and place the skewers over direct heat and close the lid. Turn the skewers every few minutes but leave the lid closed as much as possible. Cook for 12 to 15 minutes or until the pork is cooked through and the pineapple and vegetables are crisp-tender and slightly charred. Brush with some of the remaining Polynesian sauce and serve the rest on the side.

Coconut Fish Sticks

SERVINGS Makes 4 portions.

Gluten-free, Grain-free, Dairy-free, Nut-free

INGREDIENTS
1 ½	pounds tilapia fillets
1	large egg
¼	cup plus 1 teaspoon gluten-free tamari or soy sauce
2 ½	cups coconut flakes
½	cup mayonnaise

DIRECTIONS

1. Position oven racks in the top and bottom third of the oven and preheat to 400 degrees F. Line 2 baking sheets with foil and spray generously with gluten-free nonstick cooking spray.

2. Cut the tilapia fillets in half lengthwise down the center line. Halve again lengthwise, then cut in half crosswise.

3. Beat the egg in a shallow bowl with 1 teaspoon tamari. Place the coconut flakes on a plate.

4. Dip the strips of fish into the egg, shaking off the excess, then into the coconut, pressing to adhere. Place on the prepared baking sheets and spray lightly with cooking spray. Bake until golden brown and the fish feels firm to the touch, 15 to 20 minutes, rotating the baking sheets from top to bottom halfway through.

5. Whisk the remaining ¼ cup tamari with the mayonnaise. Serve the fish sticks with the sauce.

Grilled Swordfish with Orange Fennel Salad

SERVINGS Makes 4 portions.

Gluten-free, Grain-free, Dairy-free, Egg-free, Nut-free

INGREDIENTS

4	(6-ounce) swordfish fillets
¼	cup plus 2 tablespoons Asian orange sauce, divided
2	large oranges, peeled
¼	cup olive oil
1	teaspoon kosher or fine sea salt
½	teaspoon freshly ground black pepper
1	large fennel bulb, sliced

DIRECTIONS

1. Place the swordfish fillets in a large plastic storage bag. Add ¼ cup orange sauce and gently shake to coat the fillets with sauce. Marinate in the refrigerator for 30 minutes. Heat grill to medium-high (about 450 degrees F).

2. Cut the oranges into segments over a plate or bowl to catch the juice. Measure 1 tablespoon of orange juice and combine with 2 tablespoons orange sauce, olive oil, salt and pepper in a medium mixing bowl. Add the sliced fennel and toss gently to combine. Cover and refrigerate until serving time.

3. Remove swordfish from marinade and discard liquid. Brush the grates of the grill with a little bit of olive oil. Grill for 8 minutes with the lid closed, turning once.

4. Place the orange and fennel salad on plates, top with the swordfish fillets and serve.

Linguine with No-Cook Tomato Sauce

SERVINGS Makes 6 portions.

Gluten-free, Dairy-free, Egg-free, Nut-free, Refined Sugar-free, Soy-free, Vegan, Vegetarian

INGREDIENTS

20	basil leaves, plus more to serve
4	pints grape or cherry tomatoes (red, yellow or both), cut in half
1	large zucchini, cut in half lengthwise and sliced into half-moons
4	garlic cloves, minced
1	teaspoon kosher or fine sea salt, plus more to boil and taste
½	teaspoon freshly ground black pepper, plus more to taste
½	cup olive oil
1	(16-ounce) box gluten-free linguine

DIRECTIONS

1. Stack basil leaves on top of one another. Roll tightly like a cigar and thinly slice. Place the basil in a large mixing bowl with the tomatoes, zucchini, garlic, salt and pepper. Add the olive oil and stir well. Cover with plastic wrap and let sit at room temperature for at least 1 hour or up to 4 hours. You can also let it sit in the refrigerator for up to 12 hours. Let sit at room temperature while preparing the linguine.

2. Bring a large pot of heavily salted water to a boil and cook the linguine according to the package directions. Drain and add to the sauce. Toss to coat.

3. Serve with additional basil, if desired.

Simple S

ides

Pair your main dish
with its perfect mate.

Asparagus Gremolata

SERVINGS Makes 4 to 6 portions.

Gluten-free, Grain-free, Dairy-free, Egg-free, Refined Sugar-free, Soy-free, Vegan, Vegetarian

INGREDIENTS

2   tablespoons pine nuts
2   lemons, zested and juiced
2   garlic cloves, minced
¼   cup flat-leaf parsley, minced
1   pinch kosher or fine sea salt, plus more to boil
2   pounds fat asparagus spears, trimmed and peeled
2   tablespoons olive oil
1   pinch freshly ground black pepper

DIRECTIONS

1. In a small, dry skillet over medium heat, toast the pine nuts until brown and fragrant, about 5 minutes. Let cool.

2. Add the lemon zest, garlic, parsley and cooled pine nuts to a small bowl to make the gremolata. Reserve.

3. In a large skillet, bring 1 inch of lightly salted water to a boil. Add the asparagus and cook until crisp-tender, about 3 minutes. Drain water. Add the olive oil, 1 tablespoon lemon juice, salt and pepper, then toss. Transfer the asparagus to a serving plate, top with the gremolata and serve.

Cauliflower Au Gratin

SERVINGS Makes 6 portions.

*Gluten-free, Egg-free, Nut-free, Refined Sugar-free,
Soy-free, Vegetarian*

INGREDIENTS

- 1 teaspoon kosher or fine sea salt, plus more to boil
- 1 large head of cauliflower, broken into florets
- 4 tablespoons unsalted butter
- 4 tablespoons gluten-free, all-purpose flour
- 2 cups milk
- ½ teaspoon freshly ground black pepper
- 1 cup grated Gruyère cheese

DIRECTIONS

1. Preheat oven to 400 degrees F. Spray a 2-quart baking dish with gluten-free, nonstick cooking spray.

2. Bring a pot of lightly salted water to a boil. Add the cauliflower and cook until crisp-tender, about 5 minutes. Drain well.

3. In a large skillet over medium heat, melt the butter. Whisk in the flour and cook, stirring constantly for 1 minute, making sure there are no lumps. Add the milk, pepper and 1 teaspoon salt. Cook, stirring, until thickened, about 5 minutes.

4. Spread about ¼ cup of sauce in the bottom of the prepared baking dish. Add the cauliflower and top with the remaining sauce and cheese. Bake for 25 minutes, or until the sauce is bubbly and the cheese begins to brown.

Tex-Mex Skillet Corn

SERVINGS Makes 6 portions.

Gluten-free, Nut-free, Refined Sugar-free,
Soy-free, Vegetarian, Optionally Egg-free

INGREDIENTS

2	tablespoons vegetable oil
4	cups fresh or frozen corn kernels, thawed if frozen
1	(10-ounce) can gluten-free regular or hot diced tomatoes with green chilies, drained
2	tablespoons mayonnaise or vegan mayonnaise
½	cup grated Cotija cheese
½	cup fresh cilantro leaves, coarsely chopped
	Kosher or fine sea salt, to taste
	Freshly ground black pepper, to taste

DIRECTIONS

1. Heat oil in a large skillet over medium-high until hot. Add the corn kernels and cook, stirring occasionally, until they start to brown. Be careful because they pop as they cook. Add the tomatoes with chilies and cook, stirring, until any liquid has been released and evaporated, about 2 minutes.

2. Remove from heat and stir in the mayonnaise, cheese and cilantro. Season with salt and pepper, then serve.

Tofu Green Bean Stir Fry

SERVINGS Makes 6 portions.

Gluten-free, Dairy-free, Egg-free, Nut-free, Vegan, Vegetarian

INGREDIENTS
¼   cup gluten-free tamari or soy sauce
2   tablespoons gluten-free sweet chili garlic sauce
1   pound extra firm tofu, cut into ½-inch cubes
2 ½   tablespoons cornstarch
3   tablespoons vegetable oil, divided
1   pound green beans, trimmed and cut into 1-inch pieces

DIRECTIONS
1. Combine the tamari or soy sauce with the chili garlic sauce and set aside.

2. Pat the tofu dry with paper towels and transfer to a mixing bowl with the cornstarch. Toss to coat.

3. Heat 1 tablespoon of oil in a large skillet or wok over high until it starts to shimmer. Place half the tofu in an even layer in the pan. Cook the tofu undisturbed for 2 minutes. Gently flip and stir the tofu. Continue to cook and stir until the tofu is lightly golden brown on all sides, 3 to 4 minutes. Transfer the tofu to a plate and set aside. Heat 1 more tablespoon of oil in the pan and cook the remaining tofu the same way. Remove from the pan.

4. Reduce heat to medium. Add the remaining 1 tablespoon of oil and the green beans. Cook, stirring, for 1 minute. Add ¼ cup of water and continue to cook the beans for 3 minutes, or until they're bright green and crisp-tender. Increase the heat to high, add the reserved tamari chili garlic sauce mixture and boil for 1 minute, or until the sauce reduces slightly. Add the tofu and cook for 1 minute. Serve immediately.

Oven-Roasted Corn

SERVINGS Makes 6 portions.

Gluten-free, Egg-free, Nut-free, Refined Sugar-free, Soy-free, Vegetarian, Optionally Dairy-free, Optionally Vegan

INGREDIENTS

- 6 corn ears in husks
- ½ cup unsalted butter or dairy-free butter substitute, at room temperature
- 2 teaspoons chili powder
- 1 lime, zested and juiced

DIRECTIONS

1. Preheat oven to 350 degrees F. Lay the corn directly on the oven rack and roast for 30 minutes, or until soft.

2. Combine the butter with the chili powder in a small bowl. Add the lime zest and juice, then stir to combine.

3. When the corn is finished roasting, remove the husks and the corn silk. Brush with the butter mixture and serve with additional butter mixture on the side.

Scalloped Tomatoes

SERVINGS Makes 6 portions.

Gluten-free, Egg-free, Nut-free, Refined Sugar-free, Soy-free, Vegetarian

INGREDIENTS

3	pints cherry or grape tomatoes, cut in half
¼	cup plus 1 tablespoon olive oil, divided
1 ¼	teaspoons kosher or fine sea salt, divided
1	teaspoon freshly ground black pepper, divided
1 ½	cups gluten-free panko-style bread crumbs
¾	cup grated Parmesan cheese
½	cup fresh basil leaves, minced
3	garlic cloves, minced

DIRECTIONS

1. Preheat oven to 400 degrees F.

2. Put the tomatoes into a 9- by 12-inch baking dish. Top with 1 tablespoon olive oil, 1 teaspoon salt and ½ teaspoon pepper. Toss to coat.

3. In a small bowl, combine the bread crumbs, Parmesan cheese, basil, garlic, ¼ cup olive oil, ¼ teaspoon salt and ½ teaspoon pepper. Top the tomatoes with the mixture and bake for 30 minutes, or until golden brown.

Roasted Garlic Mashed Parsnips

SERVINGS Makes 4 portions.

Gluten-free, Grain-free, Egg-free, Nut-free, Refined Sugar-free, Soy-free, Vegetarian

INGREDIENTS

1	pound parsnips, peeled and diced
½	cup unsweetened almond milk
1	head roasted garlic
1	teaspoon dried parsley
2	tablespoons butter or ghee
	Kosher or fine sea salt, to taste
	Freshly ground black pepper, to taste

DIRECTIONS

1. Bring a medium saucepan of water to a boil. Add the diced parsnips and cook for approximately 10 minutes, or until soft. Drain the parsnips, transfer to a bowl, add the remaining ingredients and mash to reach desired consistency.

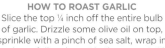

HOW TO ROAST GARLIC
Slice the top ¼ inch off the entire bulb of garlic. Drizzle some olive oil on top, sprinkle with a pinch of sea salt, wrap in aluminum foil and roast in the oven at 400 degrees F for 30 to 35 minutes. Let cool, then squeeze out the soft garlic cloves.

Smashed Minty Peas

SERVINGS Makes 4 portions.

Gluten-free, Grain-free, Egg-free, Nut-free, Refined Sugar-free, Soy-free, Vegetarian, Optionally Dairy-free, Optionally Vegan

INGREDIENTS

2	garlic cloves, peeled and smashed
1	teaspoon kosher or fine sea salt, plus more to taste
1	pound frozen peas
2	tablespoons olive oil, plus more if dairy-free
¼	cup fresh mint leaves
½	teaspoon freshly ground black pepper
2	tablespoons heavy cream (optional)

DIRECTIONS

1. Put the garlic cloves in a medium saucepan and fill it ¾ full with water. Cover the pan and bring to a boil over high heat. Once the water is boiling, remove the lid, add the salt and peas and boil just until the peas are heated through, about 2 minutes.

2. Drain the water and transfer the peas and garlic to a food processor. Add the olive oil, mint leaves and pepper and pulse a few times until blended but still chunky. Add the cream if using and pulse a couple more times. If you're not using cream, you may want to add 1 to 2 more tablespoons olive oil to give the peas a creamier texture.

3. Add more salt as needed. Return the peas to the hot pot and keep warm until serving.

NO PROCESSOR, NO PROBLEM
If you don't have a food processor, mash the peas and garlic with the olive oil, pepper and cream, if using. Mince the mint leaves and stir in.

TIME-SAVING TIP
Save time by buying packaged, pre-washed, pre-trimmed greens.

Quick Braised Greens

SERVINGS Makes 6 portions.

Gluten-free, Grain-free, Dairy-free, Egg-free, Nut-free, Refined Sugar-free, Soy-free, Optionally Vegan, Optionally Vegetarian

INGREDIENTS

2	tablespoons olive oil
4	garlic cloves, peeled and sliced
3	pounds kale, collard greens, mustard greens or a combination, thick center ribs removed and greens torn into 2- to 3-inch pieces
2	cups gluten-free, low-sodium chicken or vegetable stock
3	tablespoons balsamic vinegar
½	teaspoon crushed red pepper flakes, plus more to taste
	Kosher or fine sea salt, to taste
	Freshly ground black pepper, to taste

DIRECTIONS

1. Heat the olive oil over medium-high in a 6-quart stock pot or Dutch oven. Add the garlic and cook, stirring for 30 seconds. Add the greens in batches, adding more as they wilt down. Using tongs, turn the greens frequently to coat them with the oil and wilt them evenly. After all the greens have been added, cook for 2 minutes, stirring constantly.

2. Add the stock, vinegar and red pepper flakes. Cook, uncovered, for 15 minutes, or until the greens are tender and most of the liquid has evaporated. Add salt, pepper and more red pepper flakes, if desired.

Sautéed Spinach with Feta and Walnuts

SERVINGS Makes 4 portions.

Gluten-free, Grain-free, Egg-free, Refined Sugar-free, Soy-free, Vegetarian

INGREDIENTS

- ¼ cup walnut pieces
- 3 tablespoons olive oil, plus more to serve
- 2 shallots, minced
- 2 garlic cloves, finely minced or grated
- 1 pound baby spinach, washed and dried
- 1 ½ teaspoons kosher or fine sea salt
- ¾ teaspoon freshly ground black pepper
- ½ cup crumbled feta cheese

DIRECTIONS

1. In a small, dry skillet, toast the walnut pieces over medium heat, stirring frequently, until nuts are brown and fragrant, about 4 minutes. Reserve.

2. Heat the oil in a large, deep skillet over medium. Add the shallots and garlic and cook, stirring, until softened but not browned, about 2 minutes. Add the spinach in large handfuls, tossing constantly with tongs, until the spinach is wilted, about 2 minutes. Add the salt and pepper and toss. Remove from heat and add the reserved walnuts and feta. Drizzle with about 1 tablespoon of olive oil and serve.

Bacon and Maple Roasted Brussels Sprouts

SERVINGS Makes 6 portions.

Gluten-free, Grain-free, Dairy-free, Egg-free, Nut-free, Refined Sugar-free, Soy-free

INGREDIENTS
¼   pound gluten-free bacon, diced
1 ½   pounds Brussels sprouts, ends trimmed and cut in half
1   tablespoon olive oil
1   teaspoon kosher or fine sea salt
½   teaspoon freshly ground black pepper
2   tablespoons pure maple syrup

DIRECTIONS
1. Preheat oven to 400 degrees F. Line a rimmed baking sheet with foil.

2. Put the bacon in a medium skillet and cook over medium heat until the fat has rendered and the bacon is very crispy. Remove the bacon with a slotted spoon and drain on paper towels. Reserve 1 tablespoon of bacon fat.

3. Toss the Brussels sprouts with the reserved bacon fat, olive oil, salt and pepper. Place on the baking sheet in an even layer. Roast for 20 minutes.

4. Pour maple syrup over the sprouts, stir to coat and roast for another 5 minutes, or until the sprouts are crispy and brown on the outside and tender on the inside. Add the diced bacon to the Brussels sprouts, toss lightly to combine and serve.

Orange Chipotle Roasted Butternut Squash

SERVINGS Makes 6 portions.

Gluten-free, Grain-free, Dairy-free, Egg-free, Nut-free, Refined Sugar-free, Soy-free, Vegan, Vegetarian

INGREDIENTS

- 3 tablespoons olive oil
- ⅓ cup freshly squeezed orange juice
- ¾ teaspoon kosher or fine sea salt
- ¼ teaspoon freshly ground black pepper
- ½ teaspoon chipotle chili powder
- 1 (2-pound) butternut squash, peeled, seeded and cut into 1-inch pieces (about 5 cups)

DIRECTIONS

1. Preheat oven to 400 degrees F.

2. In a large mixing bowl, whisk together the olive oil, orange juice, salt, pepper and chili powder. Add the squash and toss well.

3. Pour the squash and liquid into a 9- by 12-inch baking dish. Spread the squash into an even layer. Bake for 35 to 40 minutes, stirring every 10 minutes, or until the squash is tender and starts to brown.

Grilled Artichokes

SERVINGS Makes 4 to 6 portions.

Gluten-free, Grain-free, Dairy-free, Nut-free, Refined Sugar-free, Soy-free, Vegetarian

INGREDIENTS

4	large artichokes
1	tablespoon water
2	lemons, quartered
1	head of garlic
	Kosher or fine sea salt, to taste
	Freshly ground black pepper, to taste
¾	cup mayonnaise

DIRECTIONS

1. Preheat grill to medium, about 350 to 400 degrees F.

2. Cut a small amount off the very top and bottom of the artichokes. Snip the sharp points off the leaves and rinse the artichokes. Cut each artichoke in quarters vertically and, with a sharp paring knife, cut the thistle out of each quarter.

3. Lay out a large piece of heavy-duty aluminum foil and put the artichoke quarters in the center. Sprinkle water over them and add the lemon quarters. Cut the top off the head and add the garlic to the foil. Sprinkle with salt and pepper and wrap the foil tightly around the whole lot. Take another large piece of foil and wrap tightly around the packet so that some steam will build up while cooking.

4. Place the artichokes on the grill, close the lid and cook over indirect heat for about 1 hour. Alternatively, you can cook the artichokes in a preheated, 400 degree F oven for 1 hour.

5. Carefully open the foil packet and transfer the artichokes and lemon wedges to a serving platter.

6. Squeeze the garlic into the mayonnaise and stir. Serve as a dipping sauce for the artichokes.

Curried Kale and Cauliflower

SERVINGS Makes 4 to 6 portions.

Gluten-free, Grain-free, Dairy-free, Egg-free, Nut-free, Refined Sugar-free, Soy-free, Vegan, Vegetarian

INGREDIENTS

2	tablespoons olive oil
10	cups chopped kale
1	head cauliflower, broken into florets
½	cup golden raisins
2	tablespoons curry powder
½	cup water
	Kosher or fine sea salt, to taste
	Freshly ground black pepper, to taste

DIRECTIONS

1. Heat the oil over medium-high in a Dutch oven or a large skillet with a lid. Add the kale (in batches, if necessary) and cook until it starts to wilt, about 2 minutes. Add the cauliflower, raisins and curry powder. Toss well to coat the vegetables with the curry powder. Add the water. Cover the pan, reduce the heat to low and cook for 15 to 20 minutes, or until the cauliflower and kale are soft.

2. Remove lid. If the water has not evaporated, raise heat to high and cook to do so, stirring constantly for 1 to 2 minutes. Season with salt and pepper, then serve.

Roasted Asparagus and Eggs

SERVINGS Makes 4 portions.

Gluten-free, Grain-free, Soy-free, Vegetarian, Optionally Dairy-free

INGREDIENTS

1	pound thick-cut asparagus
1	tablespoon olive oil
1	teaspoon kosher or fine sea salt, plus more to taste
½	teaspoon freshly ground black pepper, plus more to taste
¼	cup unsalted butter or dairy-free butter substitute, melted
¼	cup mayonnaise
1	teaspoon fresh lemon juice
2	hard-boiled eggs, peeled and sliced

DIRECTIONS

1. Preheat oven to 400 degrees F.

2. Break off the woody ends of the asparagus and peel the bottom half of the stalks with a vegetable peeler. Transfer the asparagus to a baking sheet and drizzle with olive oil. Sprinkle with salt and pepper. Roast for 25 minutes, stirring once or twice.

3. Whisk together the butter, mayonnaise and lemon juice. Drizzle the sauce over the roasted asparagus and top with sliced eggs. Sprinkle with salt and pepper, then serve.

SWEET TWIST
To make this dish even more delectable, garnish with marshmallows and craisins.

Spiced Whipped Sweet Potatoes

SERVINGS Makes 8 portions.

Gluten-free, Grain-free, Egg-free, Nut-free, Refined Sugar-free, Soy-free, Vegetarian

INGREDIENTS

4	pounds sweet potatoes
6	tablespoons unsalted butter, softened
2	teaspoons ground cinnamon
1	teaspoon chili powder
¼	cup pure maple syrup
	Kosher or fine sea salt, to taste

DIRECTIONS

1. Preheat oven to 400 degrees F. Prick the sweet potatoes all over with a fork. Transfer to a baking sheet and bake for 50 to 60 minutes, or until the potatoes are tender when pierced with a knife.

2. When cool enough to handle, cut the sweet potatoes in half and scoop the middle into a food processor fitted with the steel blade. Add the butter, cinnamon, chili powder and maple syrup. Process until creamy and smooth. Season with salt and serve warm.

Oven-Roasted Potatoes and Carrots

SERVINGS Makes 8 portions.

Gluten-free, Grain-free, Dairy-free, Egg-free, Nut-Free, Refined Sugar-free, Soy-free, Vegan, Vegetarian

INGREDIENTS

2	pounds small Yukon gold potatoes, scrubbed
8	large carrots (about 2 pounds), cut diagonally into 1-inch pieces
1	medium orange, zested and juiced
3	tablespoons olive oil
2	tablespoons finely chopped fresh rosemary
1 ½	teaspoons kosher or fine sea salt
¾	teaspoon freshly ground black pepper

DIRECTIONS

1. Preheat oven to 400 degrees F.

2. Place the potatoes and carrots in a roasting dish. Combine the orange zest and juice with the olive oil, rosemary, salt and pepper. Pour the mixture over the potatoes and carrots and toss to coat. Roast for 35 to 40 minutes, or until the potatoes and carrots are fork tender.

Scalloped Potatoes

SERVINGS Makes 8 portions.

Gluten-free, Grain-free, Egg-free, Nut-free, Refined Sugar-free, Soy-free, Vegetarian

INGREDIENTS

6	tablespoons unsalted butter, cold, plus more to prepare the baking dish
4	pounds russet potatoes, peeled and sliced ⅛-inch thick
1	tablespoon kosher or fine sea salt
1½	teaspoons freshly ground black pepper
½	teaspoon freshly ground nutmeg
2½	cups heavy cream

DIRECTIONS

1. Preheat oven to 350 degrees F. Grease a deep 3-quart baking dish with butter.

2. Fill a large bowl with ice water. Place the potato slices directly into the ice water.

3. Combine the salt, pepper and nutmeg in a bowl.

4. Dry the potatoes well and layer ¼ of the slices in the bottom of the prepared dish. Sprinkle the potatoes with ¼ of the spice mixture and dot with 2 tablespoons of butter, cut into small pieces. Repeat layering twice, then top with a final layer of potatoes and spice mixture for a total of 4 layers. Pour heavy cream evenly over the dish.

5. Bake for 1 hour. Gently press down the top layer of the potatoes with a spatula or the back of a spoon to break up the crust and allow the cream below to come to the surface.

6. Bake for another 30 to 45 minutes, or until the top is deeply browned and the potatoes are tender. Let potatoes sit for about 10 minutes, then serve.

Garlicky Grilled Potatoes

SERVINGS Makes 6 portions.

Gluten-free, Grain-free, Egg-free, Nut-free, Refined Sugar-free, Soy-free, Vegetarian

INGREDIENTS

- 2 pounds baby (¾-inch diameter) Yukon gold potatoes, washed
- 1 large white onion, halved widthwise and each half cut into 6 wedges
- 4 tablespoons unsalted butter, cut into small pieces
- 3 garlic cloves, chopped
- 1 teaspoon garlic powder
- 2 teaspoons kosher or fine sea salt
- 1 teaspoon freshly ground black pepper

DIRECTIONS

1. Heat a grill to medium, about 350 to 400 degrees F.

2. Place the potatoes in a cast-iron skillet in a single layer. Add the rest of the ingredients, stir well and cover the skillet snugly with foil. Put the pan over indirect heat and cover the grill. Cook for 30 minutes, remove foil, stir and cook uncovered for another 10 minutes, or until the potatoes are tender.

Sweet Potato Wedges with Tahini Sauce

SERVINGS Makes 6 portions.

Gluten-free, Grain-free, Dairy-free, Egg-free, Nut-free, Refined Sugar-free, Soy-free, Vegan, Vegetarian

INGREDIENTS

- 3 large (about 1 pound each) sweet potatoes, washed
- 3–4 tablespoons olive oil
- 1 ½ teaspoons kosher or fine sea salt, divided
- ¾ teaspoon freshly ground black pepper, divided
- ¼ cup tahini
- 2 tablespoons fresh lemon juice
- ½ teaspoon garlic powder
- 2–4 tablespoons water

DIRECTIONS

1. Preheat oven to 400 degrees F.

2 Slice each potato in half lengthwise, then cut each in half to form 4 quarters. Place the sweet potatoes onto a rimmed baking sheet. Drizzle with 3 tablespoons oil and sprinkle with 1 teaspoon salt and ½ teaspoon pepper. Toss well to coat, making sure that all sides of the potato wedges are coated with oil. Add another 1 tablespoon of oil, if needed. Line the wedges up, skin-side down, in a single layer on the baking dish. Roast in the top third of the oven for 35 minutes, or until the sweet potatoes start to brown and are tender.

3. While the potatoes are roasting, combine the tahini with the lemon juice, garlic powder, ½ teaspoon salt, ¼ teaspoon pepper and 2 tablespoons water in a blender or food processor. Process until creamy and pourable. Add more water, if needed.

4. Drizzle some sauce over the potatoes and serve with the rest on the side.

Quinoa Pilaf

SERVINGS Makes 4 portions.

*Gluten-free, Dairy-free, Egg-free, Refined Sugar-free,
Soy-free, Vegan, Vegetarian*

INGREDIENTS

3	teaspoons olive oil, divided
½	medium white or yellow onion, finely minced
1	cup quinoa
1	garlic clove, finely minced
1 ½	cups water
1	teaspoon kosher or fine sea salt, plus more to taste
¼	cup slivered almonds
¼	cup Italian flat leaf parsley, finely minced
	Freshly ground black pepper, to taste

DIRECTIONS

1. Heat 1 teaspoon olive oil in a large saucepan over medium. Add the onion and cook for about 2 minutes, or until the onions start to become translucent. Add the quinoa and garlic and cook for about 3 minutes, lightly toasting the quinoa while making sure the garlic doesn't brown. Add the water and salt. Raise heat, bring to a full boil, cover the pan with a lid and turn heat down to medium-low. Let simmer for about 15 minutes, or until all the liquid is absorbed and the quinoa is tender.

2. While the quinoa is simmering, toast the almond slivers in a dry skillet over high heat until they are browned and fragrant, stirring often. Watch them carefully so they do not burn. Take off the heat and set aside.

3. Remove the quinoa from the heat and let it sit in the pan, covered, for about 3 minutes. Transfer to a serving bowl and fluff with a fork. Add the parsley and toasted almonds. Drizzle with the remaining 2 teaspoons of olive oil and toss. Add salt and pepper as needed, then serve.

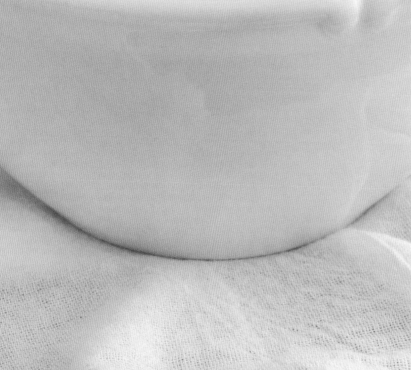

Refried Black Beans

SERVINGS Makes 6 portions.

*Gluten-free, Grain-free, Egg-free,
Nut-free, Refined Sugar-free,
Soy-free, Vegetarian, Optionally
Dairy-free, Optionally Vegan*

INGREDIENTS

2	tablespoons olive oil
2	teaspoons chili powder
1	teaspoon ground cumin
½	large white or yellow onion, diced
2	(15-ounce) cans black beans, drained and rinsed
¾	cup water, plus more as needed
	Kosher or fine sea salt, to taste
	Freshly ground black pepper, to taste
½	cup queso fresco or Monterey Jack cheese, crumbled (optional)

DIRECTIONS

1. Heat the oil in a large skillet over medium-high. Add the chili powder, cumin and onion. Cook until the onion is tender, about 5 minutes. Add the beans and water. Smash the beans with the back of a spoon or a potato masher. Cook until the beans are heated through. If they are too thick, add more water. If they are too thin, cook them a little longer. Season with salt and pepper, top with crumbled cheese, if using, and serve.

Easy Baked Beans

SERVINGS Makes 8 to 10 portions.

Gluten-free, Grain-free, Dairy-free, Egg-free, Nut-Free, Soy-free, Optionally Vegan, Optionally Vegetarian

INGREDIENTS

2   (28-ounce) cans gluten-free baked beans (with or without meat)
1   large (1 pound) sweet onion, chopped
½   cup ketchup
¾   cup spicy brown mustard
½   cup gluten-free barbecue sauce

DIRECTIONS

1. Preheat oven to 400 degrees F.

2. Combine all the ingredients in a large mixing bowl. Pour the beans into a deep 3- to 4-quart baking pan. Bake for 40 minutes, or until the beans are hot and bubbling.

Tex-Mex Skillet Mac and Cheese

SERVINGS Makes 6 portions.

Gluten-free, Egg-free, Nut-free, Refined Sugar-free, Soy-free, Vegetarian

INGREDIENTS

- 4 cups gluten-free short-cut spiral or bow tie pasta
- 1 teaspoon kosher or fine sea salt, plus more to taste
- 3 cups water
- 1 (12-ounce) can evaporated milk
- 1 (10-ounce) can diced tomatoes with green chilies, undrained
- 1 cup shredded mozzarella cheese Freshly ground black pepper, to taste

DIRECTIONS

1. Combine the pasta, salt and water in a large skillet. Bring to a boil over high heat. Cook, stirring occasionally, until nearly all of the water is gone and the pasta is tender. Add the evaporated milk and tomatoes with chilies. Bring to a boil. Reduce heat to medium and cook until the mixture thickens, about 5 minutes. Add the cheese and cook, stirring, until the cheese is melted. Add salt and pepper, then serve.

Stir-Fry Noodles with Peanut Sauce

SERVINGS Makes 6 portions.

Gluten-free, Dairy-free, Egg-free, Vegan, Vegetarian

INGREDIENTS

1	pound rice noodles (sometimes called rice sticks or Bahn Pho) or gluten-free fettuccini
	Kosher or fine sea salt, to boil
2	tablespoons vegetable oil
7	ounces shiitake mushrooms, stemmed and sliced into ¼-inch pieces
2	red bell peppers, stemmed, seeded, deveined and thinly sliced
6	green onions, white and green parts, trimmed and cut into 1-inch pieces
¾	cup gluten-free peanut sauce

DIRECTIONS

1. Cook the noodles in salted boiling water according to the package directions, stirring often with a fork to keep the noodles separated. Drain and rinse well under hot water.

2. Heat the oil over high in a large skillet or wok until it shimmers. Add the mushrooms, peppers and the white parts of the green onions. Cook for 2 minutes, stirring often. Add the drained noodles, green parts of the green onions and peanut sauce. Continue to cook, stirring constantly, for another 2 minutes, or until the noodles have absorbed most of the sauce. Serve stir fry noodles immediately.

BRANDS TO BUY
Any gluten-free peanut sauce works in this recipe, but I like San-J Thai Peanut Sauce.

Goat Cheese Polenta with Wild Mushrooms

SERVINGS Makes 4 to 6 portions.

Gluten-free, Egg-free, Nut-free, Refined Sugar-free, Soy-free, Vegetarian

INGREDIENTS

7	cups water
3	teaspoons kosher or fine sea salt, divided, plus more to taste
2	cups gluten-free polenta
8	ounces soft goat cheese, cut into pieces
4	tablespoons olive oil, divided
½	teaspoon freshly ground black pepper, plus more to taste
2	pounds assorted wild mushrooms, sliced
1	teaspoon finely chopped fresh thyme
¼	cup sherry

DIRECTIONS

1. Bring the water plus 2 teaspoons of salt to a boil. Slowly add the polenta, stirring constantly. Reduce the heat and cook, stirring occasionally, until thick, about 30 minutes. Stir in the goat cheese until melted through and creamy. Remove from heat and stir in 2 tablespoons olive oil. Add salt and pepper, as needed.

2. While the polenta is cooking, heat 2 tablespoons olive oil in a large skillet over medium. Add the mushrooms and thyme. Cook until the mushrooms have browned and released their liquid, and the liquid has evaporated, about 8 minutes. Add 1 teaspoon salt and ½ teaspoon pepper. Add the sherry and cook, stirring, until evaporated. Top the polenta with mushrooms and serve.

Easy Mexican Rice

SERVINGS Makes 6 portions.

*Gluten-free, Dairy-free, Egg-free,
Nut-free, Refined Sugar-free, Soy-free,
Vegetarian, Vegan*

INGREDIENTS

2	tablespoons olive oil
1	medium white or yellow onion, finely chopped
1	cup Arborio rice
2	(10-ounce) cans gluten-free diced tomatoes with green chilies
2	garlic cloves
½	teaspoon ground cumin
	Water, as needed

DIRECTIONS

1. Heat a large skillet over medium high. Add olive oil and onions. Cook until onion is soft but not browned, about 3 minutes. Add the rice and cook, stirring, for 2 minutes, or until the rice starts to look translucent. Transfer the mixture to a microwave-safe casserole dish with a lid.

2. Pour the tomatoes with chilies and their juice into a blender with the garlic and ground cumin and blend until smooth. Add enough water to yield 3 cups of liquid and blend.

3. Add the tomato mixture to the rice, stir and microwave on high for about 18 to 20 minutes, stirring 3 times while cooking. Remove the rice from microwave, stir, replace the lid and let stand for 5 minutes.

MICROWAVE-FREE METHOD
If not using the microwave method, then add the tomato mixture to the rice in the skillet in 1-cup increments, stirring after each addition of liquid until it is totally absorbed.

Quick Dr

inks

Cheers to a tall drink of delicious gluten-free goodness.

CHERRY LIME SPRITZER

Spatini Cocktail

SERVINGS Makes 1 cocktail.

Gluten-free, Grain-free, Dairy-free, Egg-free, Nut-free, Refined Sugar-free, Soy-free, Vegan, Vegetarian

INGREDIENTS

- 5 (1-inch long) pieces of cucumber, peeled and peel reserved to garnish
- 2 tablespoons agave nectar
- 2 tablespoons freshly squeezed lime juice
- 2 ½ ounces gin
  Ice cubes

DIRECTIONS

1. Place the cucumber, agave and lime juice in a blender and blend until fully pureed. Strain into a cocktail shaker. Add the gin and a large handful of ice. Shake well. Strain into a martini glass and garnish with a piece of cucumber peel threaded onto a toothpick or skewer.

Ginebra Gimlet

SERVINGS Makes 1 cocktail.

*Gluten-free, Grain-free, Dairy-free,
Egg-free, Nut-free, Refined Sugar-free,
Soy-free, Vegan, Vegetarian*

INGREDIENTS
- 2 ounces gin
- 1 tablespoon fresh lime juice
- 1 tablespoon agave nectar
- ½ teaspoon smoked paprika, plus more to garnish
- 1 cup ice cubes
- 1 piece of lime zest, to garnish

DIRECTIONS

1. Combine all ingredients except the lime zest in a cocktail shaker. Shake for 30 seconds or until very cold. Strain into a martini glass straight up or in a glass over ice if you prefer your cocktails on the rocks. Serve garnished with paprika and lime zest.

Mint Margarita

SERVINGS Makes 1 cocktail.

Gluten-free, Grain-free, Dairy-free, Egg-free, Nut-free, Soy-free, Vegan, Vegetarian

INGREDIENTS

- 5 tablespoons packed fresh mint leaves, divided, plus sprigs to garnish
- 2 tablespoons fresh lime juice
- 1 tablespoon agave nectar
- 1 ½ ounces silver tequila
- ½ ounce triple sec
- Ice cubes
- Kosher or margarita salt, to coat glass rim
- Limes slices, to garnish

DIRECTIONS

1. Place 4 tablespoons of whole mint leaves in the bottom of a cocktail shaker along with the lime juice and agave. Using a muddler, press down and twist repeatedly until the mint is very fragrant. Add the tequila, the triple sec and about 1 cup of ice. Shake well until very cold.

2. If desired, pour salt onto a small plate, rub a lime wedge around the rim of a glass and dip into the salt.

3. Take the remaining mint leaves, roll them up like a cigar and slice thinly with a very sharp knife. Add some ice to the glass, strain in the margarita and then stir in the sliced mint. Serve with a few slices of lime and a sprig of mint, if desired.

Ginger Beer Margaritas

SERVINGS Makes 6 cocktails.

Gluten-free, Dairy-free, Egg-free, Nut-free, Soy-free, Vegan, Vegetarian

INGREDIENTS

1	(12-ounce) container frozen limeade
1	(12-ounce) bottle gluten-free beer
1	(12-ounce) bottle ginger ale
12	ounces silver tequila
	Kosher or margarita salt, to coat glass rims
1	lime, cut into wedges
	Ice cubes

DIRECTIONS

1. Combine the limeade, beer, ginger ale and tequila in a pitcher and stir until limeade melts.

2. Pour some salt onto a small plate or saucer. Rub the rims of six glasses with lime wedges, then dip each glass into salt and coat evenly. Fill the glasses with ice, then pour the margarita mixture into each. Garnish the glasses with lime wedges and serve.

Arctic Sunset

SERVINGS Makes 1 cocktail.

Gluten-free, Dairy-free, Egg-free, Nut-free, Soy-free, Vegan, Vegetarian

INGREDIENTS

3	ounces vodka
1	ounce triple sec
	Ice cubes
1	maraschino cherry

DIRECTIONS

1. Combine the vodka and triple sec in a cocktail shaker filled with ice. Shake vigorously for at least 30 seconds, or until the cocktail is very cold. Pour the drink into a chilled martini glass, garnish with a cherry and serve.

Pineapple Margaritas

SERVINGS Makes 6 cocktails.

Gluten-free, Dairy-free, Egg-free, Nut-free, Refined Sugar-free, Soy-free, Vegan, Vegetarian

INGREDIENTS

- 1 pineapple, cut into chunks (about 3 cups)
- 8 ounces silver tequila
- ⅔ cup fresh lime juice
- ⅓ cup agave nectar
- 2 ⅔ ounces triple sec
- Ice cubes

DIRECTIONS

1. Combine the pineapple, tequila, lime juice, agave nectar and triple sec in a blender and blend on high until smooth. Serve over ice.

Skinny Cucumber Watermelon Martini

SERVINGS Makes 2 cocktails.

Gluten-free, Grain-free, Dairy-free, Egg-free, Nut-free, Soy-free, Vegetarian

INGREDIENTS

- 1 ½ cups cubed and seeded watermelon, plus more wedges to garnish
- ½ cup cubed and seeded cucumber, plus more slices to garnish
- ¼ cup orange juice
- 1 teaspoon honey
- Ice cubes
- 3 ounces Hendrick's gin

DIRECTIONS

1. In a food processor or blender, blend the watermelon, cucumber, orange juice and honey. Pour the mixture into a shaker filled with ice. Add the gin and shake well. Using a strainer, pour the mixture into two martini glasses. Garnish with watermelon and cucumber, if desired. and serve.

Almond Biscotti Martini

SERVINGS Makes 1 cocktail.

*Gluten-free, Egg-free, Soy-free,
Vegetarian*

INGREDIENTS
- 2 ounces gluten-free vanilla vodka
- ½ ounce amaretto
- ½ ounce coffee liqueur
- 1 tablespoon coffee, at room temperature
- ½ tablespoon milk

DIRECTIONS
1. Add all the ingredients to a cocktail shaker. Shake well and strain into a chilled martini glass.

Sparkling Mojitos

SERVINGS Makes 8 cocktails.

Gluten-free, Grain-free, Dairy-free, Egg-free, Nut-free, Soy-free, Optionally Vegan, Optionally Vegetarian

INGREDIENTS

- 3 limes, each cut into 6 wedges
- 1 cup fresh mint leaves, plus more to garnish
- ⅓ cup agave nectar
- 8 ounces white rum
- 2 cups ice cubes
- 1 (750-milliliter) bottle dry Prosecco, cold

DIRECTIONS

1. Combine the lime, mint and agave in a pitcher and muddle until the juice is extracted from the limes and the mixture smells minty. Add the rum and ice. Stir until the mixture is cold. Strain into another pitcher or large glass measuring cup. Mixture can be made ahead and stored in the refrigerator.

2. Fill champagne flutes halfway with the rum mixture and top with the Prosecco. Garnish with mint leaves and serve.

HIDDEN INGREDIENTS
Wine, including Prosecco, is not always vegetarian or vegan. Animal products, such as gelatin or isinglass, are often used during the filtration process, making the final product unsuitable for vegetarian and vegan diets. Certain types of beer may also be filtered this way, though the method is much less common with beer than it is with wine. If you are a vegetarian or a vegan, you should check the labels on alcohol or call the manufacturer to verify if the product is safe for your diet.

White Cosmo

SERVINGS Makes 1 cocktail.

Gluten-free, Dairy-free, Egg-free, Nut-free,
Soy-free, Vegan, Vegetarian

INGREDIENTS

	Ice cubes
1	ounce vodka
4	tablespoons white cranberry juice
1	tablespoon lime juice
½	ounce triple sec
3	frozen cranberries, to garnish

DIRECTIONS

1. Place a martini glass in the freezer for a few minutes to chill before you begin. In a cocktail shaker, add ice, vodka, cranberry juice, lime juice and triple sec. Shake well and strain into the chilled martini glass. Garnish with cranberries, if desired, and serve.

Pomosa

SERVINGS Makes 1 cocktail.

Gluten-free, Grain-free, Dairy-free, Egg-free, Nut-free, Soy-free, Optionally Vegan, Optionally Vegetarian

INGREDIENTS

4   tablespoons chilled pomegranate juice
4   ounces champagne

DIRECTIONS

1. Pour chilled pomegranate juice into a champagne flute and add champagne until the glass is full.

ALCOHOL-FREE

Cranberry Bomber

SERVINGS Makes 1 mocktail.

Gluten-free, Grain-free, Dairy-free, Egg-free, Nut-free, Soy-free, Vegetarian

INGREDIENTS
    Ice cubes
½   cup cranberry cocktail juice
1   tablespoon orange juice
2   tablespoons grenadine
½   tablespoon honey

DIRECTIONS
1. Add ice, followed by the remaining ingredients, to a cocktail shaker. Shake well until chilled. Strain into a cocktail glass and serve.

ALCOHOL-FREE

Sparkling Passionate Peach

SERVINGS Makes 1 mocktail.

Gluten-free, Grain-free, Dairy-free, Egg-free, Nut-free, Soy-free, Vegan, Vegetarian

INGREDIENTS
1	tablespoon peach puree
½	cup ice cubes
3	tablespoons sparkling apple cider
2	tablespoons passion fruit puree

DIRECTIONS

1. Pour the peach puree into a champagne flute.

2. Add the remaining ingredients to a blender and blend until the ice is gone and the mixture is smooth. Pour the blended mixture over the peach puree. Stir the cocktail until all the ingredients are well combined.

Cherry Lime Spritzer

SERVINGS Makes 8 mocktails.

Gluten-free, Grain-free, Dairy-free, Egg-free, Nut-free, Soy-free, Vegan, Vegetarian

INGREDIENTS

¼	cup fresh mint leaves, thinly sliced
¾	cup sugar (more or less to taste)
¾	cup freshly squeezed lime juice (6–8 limes)
½	cup maraschino cherry juice
2	liters cold club soda
	Ice cubes
8	maraschino cherries, to garnish
1	large lime, cut into 8 thin slices, to garnish
8	sprigs fresh mint, to garnish

DIRECTIONS

1. In a large pitcher, mash together the sliced mint leaves, sugar, lime juice and maraschino cherry juice with a wooden spoon. Refrigerate until serving time.

2. Before serving, add the club soda and stir. Pour over ice into glasses and garnish with cherries, lime slices and mint.

ALCOHOL-FREE

Garden Party Lemonade

SERVINGS Makes 6 to 8 mocktails.

Gluten-free, Grain-free, Dairy-free, Egg-free, Nut-free, Soy-free, Vegan, Vegetarian

INGREDIENTS

1	cup freshly squeezed lemon juice (5–6 lemons)
1	seedless cucumber, peeled and chopped
2	sprigs fresh dill, roughly chopped
¾–1	cup sugar
	Ice cubes, crushed
4	cups water
	Lemon slices, to garnish
	Dill sprigs. to garnish
	Cucumber spears, to garnish

DIRECTIONS

1. Put lemon juice, cucumber, dill, ¾ cup sugar, 1 cup ice and about 1 cup of water in a blender. Blend for about a minute. Pour into a pitcher and mix with the rest of the water.

2. Add more sugar, if desired. If you decide to add more sugar, pour some of the lemonade into the blender, add the sugar and blend for a few seconds. Stir the liquid from the blender back into the mixture.

3. Pour over ice, garnish with lemon slices, dill sprigs and cucumber spears, if desired, and serve.

Sweet Tr

eats

From sugary sweet to sugar-free, these tasty desserts are to-die-for.

DAIRY-FREE CHOCOLATE FONDUE

Chocolate-Covered Pretzels

SERVINGS Makes 10 to 12 portions.

Gluten-free, Egg-free, Vegetarian, Optionally Dairy-free, Optionally Vegan

INGREDIENTS
1   (14-ounce) bag gluten-free pretzel twists
1   cup semisweet chocolate chips or dairy-free semisweet chocolate chips
1   cup slivered almonds, chopped

DIRECTIONS
1. Line 2 baking sheets with parchment or waxed paper. Place the pretzels on the paper close to each other, saving any broken pretzels for another use.

2. Melt the chocolate chips in a microwave for 1 minute to 1 minute 30 seconds, or in a bowl over barely simmering water until most of the chips are melted. Stir until the chocolate is smooth and glossy. Scrape the chocolate into a small plastic food storage bag. Cut off the tip of one of the corners of the bag and drizzle the chocolate back and forth over the pretzels. Sprinkle the chocolate with the chopped almonds.

3. Transfer the baking sheets to the refrigerator for 1 hour, or until the chocolate is firm. The pretzels can be made 1 day ahead and stored, covered, in the refrigerator.

Dairy-Free Chocolate Fondue

SERVINGS Makes 6 to 8 portions.

Gluten-free, Dairy-free, Egg-free, Nut-free, Soy-free, Vegan, Vegetarian

INGREDIENTS

- 1 (12-ounce) bag dairy-free semisweet chocolate chips
- 1 (13 ½-ounce) can full-fat coconut milk
- 1 tablespoon pure vanilla extract
- 1 tablespoon gluten- and dairy-free chocolate liqueur or strong coffee
Berries or sliced fruit, to serve
Gluten-free cookies, to serve

DIRECTIONS

1. In a heavy saucepan over medium heat, melt the chocolate with the coconut milk. Stir constantly until thickened, about 5 minutes. Remove from heat and stir in the vanilla and liqueur.

2. Transfer the chocolate to a fondue pot and serve warm with fruit or cookies to dip.

Dairy-Free Fudge Pops

SERVINGS Makes 6 to 8 pops.

Gluten-free, Dairy-free, Egg-free, Nut-free, Refined Sugar-free, Soy-free, Vegan, Vegetarian

INGREDIENTS

1	(13 ½-ounce) can full-fat coconut milk, divided
2	teaspoons cornstarch
¾	cup agave nectar
½	cup unsweetened cocoa powder
2	teaspoons pure vanilla extract

DIRECTIONS

1. Shake the coconut milk well and combine ¼ cup with cornstarch. Set aside.

2. In a medium saucepan, whisk together the remaining coconut milk, agave and cocoa powder. Bring to a simmer over medium heat, whisking frequently. Add the cornstarch mixture, raise the heat and bring to a boil, stirring constantly. Continue to cook for 1 minute after the mixture starts to boil. Remove the mixture from heat and stir in the vanilla. Strain into a clean pitcher or large glass measuring cup and let cool to room temperature.

3. Pour the cooled mixture into popsicle molds, add popsicle sticks and freeze until firm, about 5 hours.

4. To release the fudge pops from their molds, you might need to submerge them into hot water for a few seconds.

Almost-Instant Chocolate Mousse

SERVINGS Makes 6 portions.

Gluten-free, Nut-free, Soy-free, Vegetarian

INGREDIENTS

1 ½   cups marshmallow creme or fluff
1 ½   cups semisweet or bittersweet
      chocolate chips
¼   cup water
1   cup heavy whipping cream
1   teaspoon pure vanilla extract

DIRECTIONS

1. Combine the marshmallow creme, chocolate chips and water in a heavy saucepan over low heat.

2. Cook gently, stirring occasionally, until the creme and chocolate are melted and smooth. Remove from heat and let cool.

3. Whip the heavy cream with the vanilla until thick, soft peaks form. Fold the cream into the chocolate mixture until fully combined. Spoon the mousse into small dessert dishes and chill for about 5 minutes or up to 24 hours.

Mudslide Pie

SERVINGS Makes 8 portions.

Gluten-free, Egg-free, Nut-free, Soy-free, Vegetarian

INGREDIENTS

22	gluten-free chocolate sandwich cookies, divided
¼	cup butter, melted
6	cups coffee-flavored ice cream, softened
½	cup heavy whipping cream, whipped
¼	cup gluten-free caramel syrup

DIRECTIONS

1. Place 19 cookies in a food processor fitted with the steel blade. Process until ground into fine crumbs. Add the melted butter and pulse several times to combine. Pour the mixture into a 9-inch deep-dish pie pan and press firmly and evenly on the bottom and up the sides of the pan. Freeze for 15 minutes.

2. Spread the ice cream into the frozen crust and smooth the top. Freeze for at least 4 hours or up to two days.

3. Coarsely crush the remaining 3 cookies. Spread the whipped cream over the ice cream layer, sprinkle with crushed cookies and drizzle with caramel syrup. Serve immediately or store in the freezer until ready to eat.

No-Bake Pistachio Chocolate Truffle Cake

SERVINGS Makes 10 to 12 portions.

*Gluten-free, Grain-free, Egg-free, Soy-free, Vegetarian,
Optionally Dairy-free, Optionally Vegan*

INGREDIENTS

- 1   (12-ounce) semisweet, bittersweet or dairy-free dark chocolate baking bar
- 1   cup heavy whipping cream or full-fat coconut milk (shaken well before measured)
- 3   tablespoons gluten-free coffee-flavored liqueur (optional)
- 1   teaspoon pure vanilla extract
- ⅓   cup roasted, salted and shelled pistachios, coarsely chopped

DIRECTIONS

1. Spray an 8- by 4-inch loaf pan with cooking spray or brush with butter. Line the pan with a piece of parchment paper.

2. Chop the chocolate evenly into small pieces. Alternatively, you can use good quality chocolate chips that contain no wax fillers. Place the chocolate in a mixing bowl.

3. Bring the cream and liqueur (if using) just to a boil over medium-high heat. Stir the vanilla into the hot cream. Pour over the chocolate and let sit for 5 minutes. Stir until the chocolate and cream are fully combined and the mixture is smooth and glossy. Pour into the prepared pan, smooth out the top and sprinkle with the chopped nuts. Cover with a piece of plastic wrap and refrigerate 4 hours, or until firm.

4. Using the parchment to help you, remove the cake from the pan and slice with a thin, hot knife (run the knife under hot water then dry it with a towel before slicing the cake).

Chocolate Cherry Dump Cake

SERVINGS Makes 10 to 12 portions.

Gluten-free, Egg-free, Soy-free, Vegetarian

INGREDIENTS
1   (27-ounce) jar cherry pie filling
1   (15-ounce) box gluten-free chocolate cake mix
1   cup butter, cut into slices
1   cup sliced almonds

DIRECTIONS

1. Preheat oven to 375 degrees F. Pour the cherry pie filling into a 9-by 13-inch baking dish and spread evenly in the pan. Sprinkle the chocolate cake mix over cherries. Distribute the butter over the top of the cake mix. Sprinkle on the sliced almonds and bake for 1 hour, or until the crust is set and the cherry mixture is hot and bubbly. Serve warm.

Dairy-Free Chocolate Pots

SERVINGS Makes 6 portions.

Gluten-free, Grain-free, Dairy-free, Nut-free, Soy-free, Vegetarian

INGREDIENTS

- 1 (13 ½-ounce) can full-fat coconut milk
- 1 (9-ounce) bag dairy-free dark chocolate, chopped, or 1 ½ cups dairy-free chocolate chips
- 1 teaspoon pure vanilla extract
- 1 large egg, lightly beaten
  Berries, to garnish

DIRECTIONS

1. Bring 2 inches of water to a simmer in a large saucepan. Turn the heat to low and keep the water at barely a simmer.

2. Shake the coconut milk well and pour into a heatproof mixing bowl that will fit over the saucepan without the bottom touching the simmering water. Add the chocolate to the bowl with the milk and place over the sauce pan. Melt the chocolate, stirring a few times. Once melted, whisk in the vanilla, followed by the egg. Continue whisking over the heat until the mixture is smooth.

3. Transfer the mixture from the bowl into a pitcher or spouted measuring cup for easy pouring, then pour into six small tea cups or ramekins. Chill for at least 3 or up to 24 hours.

4. Garnish with fresh berries, if desired.

Strawberry Fool

SERVINGS Makes 10 to 12 portions.

*Gluten-free, Grain-free, Egg-free,
Soy-free, Vegetarian, Optionally Dairy-free*

INGREDIENTS

1	pint fresh strawberries, hulled and sliced
½	cup sugar
1	cup heavy whipping cream, whipped, or 2 cups dairy-free whipped topping
¼	cup shelled pistachios, chopped

DIRECTIONS

1. Mash the strawberries in a saucepan with a potato masher or the back of a spoon. Add the sugar and cook on medium heat for 5 minutes. Pour the mixture into a bowl and refrigerate until cold, about 30 minutes.

2. Fold the cooled strawberries into the whipped cream, leaving the mixture streaky. Spoon into shot glasses or small glasses and sprinkle with chopped pistachios. Strawberry fool can be made 1 day ahead and kept refrigerated until time to serve.

Blueberry Fool

SERVINGS Makes 4 portions.

*Gluten-free, Grain-free, Egg-free,
Nut-free, Soy-free, Vegetarian*

INGREDIENTS
3   cups fresh or frozen blueberries,
    thawed if frozen, divided
2–3 tablespoons agave nectar or sugar,
    depending on sweetness of berries
1 ¼ cups heavy whipping cream, divided

DIRECTIONS
1. Reserve 1 cup berries to layer
and garnish. Place the remaining
berries along with the agave
or sugar in a blender or food
processor and puree until smooth.
Whip the cream until stiff peaks
form. Reserve some whipped
cream to garnish. Fold the puree
into the remaining whipped
cream until almost all the streaks
are gone.

2. Spoon half the blueberry cream
mixture into 4 serving dishes,
top with some blueberries and
the remaining blueberry cream
mixture. Garnish with reserved
cream and remaining berries.
Serve immediately or refrigerate
for up to 30 minutes.

Limoncello Syllabub

SERVINGS Makes 6 portions.

Gluten-free, Egg-free, Nut-Free, Soy-free, Vegetarian

INGREDIENTS
- 3 large lemons, divided
- ¾ cup powdered sugar
- 1 ½ cups heavy whipping cream
- 6 tablespoons limoncello
- 6 mint sprigs, to garnish

DIRECTIONS

1. Finely zest and juice 2 lemons. Sift the powdered sugar into the cream and beat with a mixer until mixture starts to thicken. Add the lemon zest, lemon juice and limoncello. Whip until thick.

2. Spoon the mixture into small dessert bowls or glasses and chill for at least 30 minutes or up to 24 hours.

3. Cut the remaining lemon into 6 slices and garnish the syllabub with lemon and mint.

Pineapple Coconut Pops

SERVINGS Makes 10 pops.

Gluten-free, Grain-free, Dairy-free, Egg-free, Nut-free, Soy-free, Vegan, Vegetarian, Optionally Refined Sugar-free

INGREDIENTS

4 ½   cups chopped fresh pineapple
1   cup coconut milk
¾   cup sugar or coconut palm sugar

DIRECTIONS

1. Place all ingredients in a blender and process until smooth. Strain the mixture through a fine sieve. Pour into popsicle molds and freeze for 3 hours, or until solid.

Chocolate- and Pistachio-Covered Strawberries

SERVINGS Makes 8 to 12 portions.

Gluten-free, Grain-free, Dairy-free,
Egg-free, Soy-free, Vegan, Vegetarian

INGREDIENTS

⅓ cup finely chopped pistachios

8 ounces dairy-free bittersweet or semisweet chocolate chips

1 tablespoon vegetable shortening

1 pound large strawberries with stems, washed and dried well

DIRECTIONS

1. Line a sheet pan with parchment or waxed paper. Place the pistachios in a small bowl.

2. Bring a pot of water to a boil. Combine the chocolate and shortening in a heatproof bowl. Set the bowl over the pot of simmering water, making sure the bottom of the bowl does not touch the water. Stir until the chocolate is melted and smooth. Remove from heat.

3. Hold the strawberries by the stems and dip them into chocolate. Lift and twist the berries slightly, letting the excess chocolate drip off. Dip the strawberries into the nuts. Place the strawberries on the prepared baking sheet and refrigerate until the chocolate is hard, about 1 hour.

SEMIFREDDO EXPLAINED
Semifreddo, which translates to "half-cold" in Italian, is a sliceable dessert similar to ice cream or gelato. Don't be intimidated by this dish: The only thing difficult about it is the name.

Honey
Semifreddo

SERVINGS Makes 6 to 8 portions.

Gluten-free, Grain-free, Refined Sugar-free, Soy-free, Vegetarian, Optionally Dairy-free

INGREDIENTS
1	large egg
4	large egg yolks
½	cup plus 3 tablespoons honey, divided
1 ¼	cups heavy whipping cream or coconut cream
¼	cup sliced almonds, toasted

DIRECTIONS

1. Line a 9-inch loaf pan with plastic wrap. Bring a pot of water to a simmer. Place the egg, egg yolks and ½ cup honey in a heatproof bowl. Place the bowl over the simmering water, making sure the bottom of the bowl does not touch the water. With a handheld mixer, beat the mixture until pale yellow and thick. Remove from heat and let cool.

2. Whip the cream or coconut cream until thick peaks form. Fold the cream into the honey mixture. Transfer to the prepared loaf pan and freeze for at least 3 hours or up to 3 days.

3. Turn the semifreddo out onto a rectangular platter when ready to serve. Drizzle with remaining honey and sprinkle with almonds. Cut into slices and serve.

Quick "Baked" Apples

SERVINGS Makes 6 portions.

Gluten-free, Grain-free, Egg-free, Soy-free, Vegetarian, Optionally Dairy-free, Optionally Vegan

INGREDIENTS
- ¼ cup chopped walnuts
- 3 large tart apples, halved and cored
- 3 tablespoons unsalted butter or dairy-free butter substitute
- 6 tablespoons packed brown sugar
- ¼ cup dried cranberries

DIRECTIONS

1. Place the walnuts in a small dry skillet and toast over medium heat until browned and fragrant, about 5 minutes. Reserve.

2. Make a 1-inch-wide well in the center of each apple and place them in a microwave-safe baking dish. Add ½ tablespoon butter to the center of each apple half. Divide the brown sugar and dried cranberries among the apples. Cover the dish with plastic wrap and microwave on high power for 3 minutes 30 seconds, or until tender. Let cool for 2 minutes, top with reserved walnuts and serve.

Butternut Squash Pudding

SERVINGS Makes 6 portions.

Gluten-free, Grain-free, Nut-free, Refined Sugar-free, Soy-free, Vegetarian, Optionally Dairy-free

INGREDIENTS

- 1 large (2 ¼–2 ½ pound) butternut squash, halved and seeded
- 1 cup water
- 1 (14-ounce) can full-fat coconut milk
- 4 large eggs
- ½ cup pure maple syrup
- ½ teaspoon kosher or fine sea salt
  Whipped cream or dairy-free whipped topping, to serve (optional)

DIRECTIONS

1. Preheat oven to 350 degrees F. Place cut side of the butternut squash down on a rimmed baking sheet and add water. Bake until the squash is fork tender, 30 to 35 minutes. Reduce the oven temperature to 325 degrees F.

2. Scrape the middle from the cooked squash and place it in the blender. Puree until smooth, scraping down the sides of the blender as needed. Add the coconut milk, eggs, maple syrup and salt. Blend the mixture until smooth.

3. Pour the mixture into a 1-quart baking dish and place the baking dish in a roasting pan. Fill the roasting pan with boiling water to reach halfway up the side of the baking dish. Bake for 1 hour.

4. Cool completely. Serve with whipped cream or dairy-free whipped topping, if desired.

Chocolate Chip Cookies

SERVINGS Makes 24 cookies.

Gluten-free, Grain-free, Soy-free, Vegetarian, Optionally Dairy-free, Optionally Nut-free

INGREDIENTS

- 1 cup creamy peanut or sunflower seed butter
- 1 cup semisweet or dairy-free chocolate chips
- 1 cup packed brown sugar
- 2 large eggs
- 1 tablespoon pure vanilla extract

DIRECTIONS

1. Preheat oven to 350 degrees F. Line 2 baking sheets with parchment paper or silicone baking mats.

2. Combine all the ingredients in a large mixing bowl and stir well. Drop tablespoonfuls of batter onto the prepared baking sheets. Flatten gently with a spatula.

3. Bake for 10 to 12 minutes. Let cool slightly and serve.

Coffee Cocoa Almond Macaroons

SERVINGS Makes 36 cookies.

Gluten-free, Grain-free, Soy-free, Vegetarian, Optionally Dairy-free

INGREDIENTS

2	(8-ounce) cans gluten-free almond paste (not marzipan)
1	large egg white
1	cup powdered sugar, divided
½	teaspoon kosher or fine sea salt
¼	cup coffee liqueur
1	tablespoon unsweetened cocoa powder

DIRECTIONS

1. Line 2 baking sheets with parchment paper or silicone baking mats. Preheat oven to 350 degrees F.

2. Place the almond paste and egg white in the bowl of a mixer fitted with the whisk attachment. Beat until smooth, about 2 minutes. Sift in ½ cup powdered sugar. Add the salt and coffee liqueur and beat, starting on low and gradually increasing speed to medium until fully combined, about 1 more minute.

3. In a small mixing bowl, whisk together the remaining ½ cup powdered sugar and cocoa powder, making sure to break up any lumps. Scoop the dough with a #60 ice cream scoop to form 1-tablespoon balls and drop 3 or 4 balls of dough into the sugar-cocoa powder mixture. Roll the dough to thoroughly coat with the sugar mixture and place on the prepared baking sheets. Continue until all the cookie dough is used.

4. Bake for 15 minutes. Let the cookies cool completely on the pans, then serve.

NUT-FREE COOKIES
To make these nut-free, substitute peanut butter with sunflower seed butter and add ¼ teaspoon of fresh lemon juice. The juice will prevent the cookies from turning slightly green due to the natural chlorophyll in the sunflower seeds.

Peanut Butter Cookies

SERVINGS Makes 16 cookies.

Gluten-free, Grain-free, Dairy-free, Soy-free, Vegetarian, Optionally Nut-free

INGREDIENTS

- 1 cup creamy peanut butter
- 1 cup sugar, plus more to roll
- 1 large egg, lightly beaten
- 1 teaspoon baking powder
- 1 teaspoon pure vanilla extract

DIRECTIONS

1. Preheat oven to 350 degrees F. Line 2 baking sheets with parchment paper or silicone baking mats.

2. In a large bowl, combine the peanut butter with the sugar, stirring until fully combined. Add the egg, baking powder and vanilla and stir well.

Pour additional sugar into a small bowl or onto a plate.

3. Form the mixture into 16 walnut-sized balls. Place each ball of dough into the sugar and roll to completely coat with sugar. Place on the prepared baking sheet, spacing the cookies 3 inches apart.

4. Using the tines of a fork dipped in sugar, gently press each dough ball to flatten. Turn the fork 90 degrees and gently press again to make the crosshatch markings of a peanut butter cookie.

5. Bake the cookies for 12 to 14 minutes, or until set and golden brown. Let the cookies cool on the baking sheet for about 5 minutes, then gently transfer the cookies with a spatula to a wire rack to cool completely.

No-Bake Coconut Snowball Cookies

SERVINGS Makes 48 cookies.

Gluten-free, Egg-free, Nut-free, Soy-free, Vegetarian, Optionally Dairy-free, Optionally Vegan

INGREDIENTS

2	(13 ½-ounce) cans full-fat coconut milk
⅔	cup agave nectar
⅛	teaspoon kosher or fine sea salt
3	cups gluten-free graham-style cracker crumbs
2	cups semisweet or dairy-free chocolate chips
3	cups coconut flakes

DIRECTIONS

1. Combine the coconut milk, agave and salt in a large saucepan with high sides. Use a saucepan that is larger than you think you will need to keep the mixture from boiling over. Bring to a boil over high heat. Adjust the temperature to keep the mixture boiling but not boiling over and let boil for 30 minutes, or until the mixture has reduced to about 1 ¾ cups and is a light amber color. You can check by pouring the mixture into a heatproof measuring cup. If it has not reduced enough, just boil a little longer. Let cool and refrigerate for about 30 minutes.

2. Line 2 baking sheets with parchment or waxed paper.

3. Combine the cooled coconut milk mixture with the gluten-free graham-style cracker crumbs in a large mixing bowl and stir. Stir in the chocolate chips. Pour the coconut flakes into a bowl or onto a plate.

4. For each cookie, drop about 1 tablespoon of the cookie mixture into the coconut flakes and roll into a ball. A small #60 ice cream scoop works well to measure the dough. Place the dough on the prepared pans and repeat with the remaining mixture.

5. Put the cookies in the refrigerator until hardened, about 30 minutes.

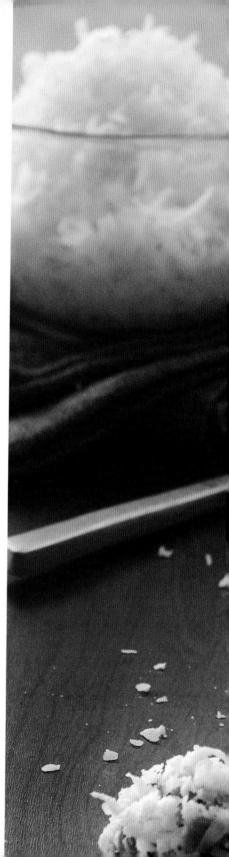

Pignoli Cookies

SERVINGS Makes 36 cookies.

*Gluten-free, Grain-free, Dairy-free,
Soy-free, Vegetarian*

INGREDIENTS
- 1 (8-ounce) can gluten-free almond paste (not marzipan)
- 1 cup sugar
- 1 pinch of kosher or fine sea salt
- 2 large egg whites
- ¼ cup pine nuts

DIRECTIONS

1. Preheat oven to 350 degrees F. Line two baking sheets with parchment paper or silicone baking mats.

2. Break almond paste into small pieces and transfer to the bowl of a food processor. Process until almost smooth. With the processor running, gradually add the sugar through the feed tube. Turn off the processor, add salt and egg whites, then process until it turns into a batter. Using a #60 ice cream scoop or a spoon, drop 1-tabelspoon balls of dough onto prepared pans, spacing about 2 inches apart. Press 3 to 4 nuts onto each cookie.

3. Bake about 15 minutes or until cookies are firm and lightly browned. Let cool on pans for 5 minutes, then remove to a wire rack to cool completely.

Peanut Butter and Jelly Ice Cream Sandwiches

SERVINGS Makes 8 sandwiches.

Gluten-free, Grain-free, Soy-free, Vegetarian, Optionally Dairy-free, Optionally Nut-free

INGREDIENTS
- 1 quart strawberry or any flavor ice cream or dairy-free ice cream
- ¾ cup strawberry or any flavor jam or jelly
- 16 gluten-free Peanut Butter Cookies (page 231)

DIRECTIONS

1. Remove the ice cream from the freezer and let sit at room temperature to soften for about 5 minutes.

2. Spread a layer of jam on the flat side of each peanut butter cookie. Place a scoop of ice cream on eight of the cookies. Top with the remaining cookies, jam side down. Gently squeeze the cookies together until the ice cream and jam come to the edges of the cookies. Put the ice cream sandwiches in the freezer for at least 30 minutes, then serve. The sandwiches can also be made several days ahead and stored in the freezer in a large plastic food storage bag.

TIN TIP
This recipe works best with silicone baking pans, as it makes removing the s'mores easier. If you only have metal muffin pans, line them with paper cupcake liners.

Frozen S'Mores

SERVINGS Makes 6 s'mores.

Gluten-free, Egg-free, Soy-free, Vegetarian, Optionally Dairy-free, Optionally Vegan

INGREDIENTS

1 ½	pints rocky road or chocolate ice cream or dairy-free ice cream
1 ¼	cups gluten-free graham-style cracker crumbs
2	tablespoons melted unsalted butter or dairy-free butter substitute
8	teaspoons mini semisweet chocolate chips or dairy-free chocolate chips, divided
½	cup heavy whipping cream or 1 cup dairy-free whipped topping

DIRECTIONS

1. Spray a 6-count silicone muffin pan with gluten-free, nonstick cooking spray or brush lightly with oil.

2. Let the ice cream soften at room temperature for about 10 minutes or microwave on high for 30 seconds so the ice cream is easy to scoop.

3. Combine the gluten-free graham-style crumbs and melted butter until fully mixed. Place a heaping tablespoon into each cup of the muffin pan and press down firmly. Reserve the remaining crumbs to garnish. Sprinkle 1 teaspoon of chocolate chips into the bottom of each cup on top of the crust. Reserve the remaining chips for garnish. Scoop ice cream into each cup, filling to the top, and press down firmly with the bottom of a glass. Freeze until firm, 1 to 2 hours.

4. If using heavy cream, whip until stiff peaks form. Remove the s'mores from the muffin pan by pushing on the bottom of each muffin cup and popping them out. Top with whipped cream, garnish with the remaining crumbs and chocolate chips and serve.

Vanilla Chocolate Cherry Mini Milkshakes

SERVINGS Makes 6 shakes.

Gluten-free, Grain-free, Egg-free, Nut-free, Soy-free, Vegetarian

INGREDIENTS
- 1 cup heavy whipping cream
- 2 (1.55-ounce) chocolate bars, finely chopped
- 18 maraschino cherries, divided
- 1 quart vanilla bean ice cream, slightly softened
- ¾ cup milk

DIRECTIONS

1. Whip the cream until stiff peaks form, then refrigerate until ready to serve.

2. Remove stems from 12 cherries and chop finely.

3. Put the ice cream and milk in a blender and process until thick and smooth. Add the chopped chocolate and cherries and blend. Pour the mixture into the prepared glasses, top with whipped cream and cherries and serve with a straw and a spoon.

PRETTY PRESENTATION
Decorate serving glasses with chocolate. To do so, hold an 8-ounce glass or jar sideways, squirt in about 1 tablespoon of chocolate syrup about ¼ of the way down from the top and rotate the glass to coat the inside. Transfer the glasses to the freezer until ready to serve.

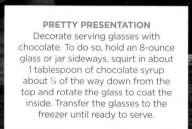

Salted Caramel Pots de Crème

SERVINGS Makes 6 portions.

Gluten-free, Grain-free, Nut-free, Refined Sugar-free, Soy-free, Vegetarian

INGREDIENTS

- ¾ cup agave nectar
- 2 cups heavy whipping cream
- 6 large egg yolks
- ½ teaspoon kosher or fine sea salt

DIRECTIONS

1. Bring the agave to a boil in a large saucepan with high sides, using a larger pan than you think you will need. Let boil for 1 minute, carefully add the cream and cook for 1 minute, just to heat.

2. Whisk the egg yolks in a bowl. Ladle in about 1 ¼ cups of the warm cream mixture and stir. Add the eggs to the cream, whisk together, and cook, stirring, until thick enough to coat the back of a spoon, about 5 minutes.

3. Pour the mixture through a fine mesh strainer into a pitcher and pour into small bowls, tea cups or ramekins. Refrigerate for 4 hours, or until firm. Sprinkle each serving with a little salt and serve.

No Bake, Cookies-and-Cream Cheesecakes

SERVINGS Makes 12 cheesecakes.

Gluten-free, Egg-free, Nut-free, Soy-free, Vegetarian

INGREDIENTS
- 21   gluten-free chocolate sandwich cookies, divided
- 1   cup heavy whipping cream
- 1   (8-ounce) package cream cheese, softened
- ½   cup sugar
- 1   teaspoon pure vanilla extract

DIRECTIONS

1. Place paper liners in cups of a 12-count muffin pan.

2. Take 3 cookies, cut them in quarters to garnish, and set aside. Place 12 cookies in a plastic freezer bag and pound them with a rolling pin until they turn into fine crumbs. Divide the crumbs among the muffin cups and press down very firmly and evenly. Place the remaining cookies in the bag and break until bigger pieces of cookie and crumbs remain.

3. Whip the cream with a hand mixer on high speed until stiff peaks form. Place the cream cheese, sugar and vanilla in a large mixing bowl and beat on high speed until smooth and well blended. Fold in the whipped cream and the crushed cookie pieces. Spoon the mixture into the muffin cups. Place one of the quartered cookies on top of each cheesecake. Refrigerate until serving, at least 5 minutes or up to 24 hours ahead.

Key Lime Pie

SERVINGS Makes 8 portions.

Gluten-free, Nut-free, Soy-free, Vegetarian

INGREDIENTS

1   (8-ounce) package cream cheese, at room temperature
1   (14-ounce) can sweetened condensed milk
3   large egg yolks
½   cup fresh key lime or lime juice
1   pre-made gluten-free graham cracker crust

DIRECTIONS

1. Preheat oven to 350 degrees F.

2. In the bowl of an electric mixer, preferably fitted with a paddle attachment, beat cream cheese until smooth and creamy. Add the sweetened condensed milk and egg yolks and beat until fully incorporated, scraping down the sides of the bowl as needed. Add the lime juice and beat well.

3. Pour the mixture into the crust and smooth the top with a spatula. Place the pie on a baking sheet and cook for 10 minutes, or until filling begins to set. Let cool completely.

4. Refrigerate for at least 2 or up to 24 hours before serving.

Quick Mango Sorbet

SERVINGS Makes 1 portion.

Gluten-free, Grain-free, Dairy-free, Egg-free, Nut-free, Refined Sugar-free, Soy-free, Vegan, Vegetarian

INGREDIENTS
1 ½   cups frozen mango chunks
½   lime, juiced
       Water, as needed
       Chili powder (optional)

DIRECTIONS
1. Add the mango chunks and lime juice to a blender. Pulse a few times until the mixture is the consistency of granita. Add water, 1 tablespoon at a time, until the sorbet is creamy but still frozen, or soft-set frozen. Spoon into a martini glass or bowl, sprinkle with chili powder, if desired, and serve immediately.

Pomegranate Semifreddo

SERVINGS Makes 6 portions.

Gluten-free, Grain-free, Egg-free, Nut-free, Soy-free, Vegetarian

INGREDIENTS

¾	cup pomegranate juice
1	lime, juiced
1¼	cups powdered sugar
2	cups heavy whipping cream
	Seeds from 1 fresh pomegranate, to garnish

DIRECTIONS

1. Whisk together pomegranate juice, lime juice and powdered sugar until the sugar is dissolved. Add cream and whisk (either by hand or with a hand mixer) until soft pink peaks begin to form.

2. Spoon mixture into a plastic or glass container with a snug lid, smooth to compact and freeze for at least 4 hours or overnight.

3. Serve with fresh pomegranate seeds to garnish, if desired.

Tropical Dairy-Free No-Churn Ice Cream

SERVINGS Makes 2 to 3 portions.

Gluten-free, Grain-free, Dairy-free, Egg-free, Nut-free, Soy-free, Vegan, Vegetarian

INGREDIENTS

1	(15-ounce) can cream of coconut
¾	cup mango nectar
¾	cup powdered sugar

DIRECTIONS

1. Refrigerate the cream of coconut and mango nectar overnight. Place a large mixing bowl and beaters in the freezer for about 5 minutes before making.

2. Put the cold cream of coconut into the cold mixing bowl and add powdered sugar. (The cream of coconut will be partially solidified at the top and watery at the bottom. This is normal, as the cream rises to the top and solidifies.) Beat on high speed until the cream of coconut is very thick, like lightly whipped cream. Add the mango nectar and mix until well blended. Spoon the mixture into a plastic or glass container with a snug lid, smooth to compact and freeze for at least 8 hours or overnight.

3. The ice cream will be a soft (not solid) frozen mixture. For best results, serve in cold dishes or coconut halves that have been placed in the freezer for a couple hours.

Index

MUDSLIDE PIE
PAGE 215

Media Lab Books
For inquiries, call 646-838-6637

Copyright 2016 Topix Media Lab

Published by Topix Media Lab
14 Wall Street, Suite 4B
New York, NY 10005

Printed in China

The information in this book has been carefully researched, and every reasonable effort has been made to ensure its accuracy. Neither the book's publisher nor its creators assume any responsibility for any accidents, injuries, losses or other damages that might come from its use. You are solely responsible for taking any and all reasonable and necessary precautions when performing the activities detailed in its pages.

All rights reserved. No part of this book may be reproduced in any form or by any electronic or mechanical means, including information storage and retrieval systems, without permission in writing from the publisher, except by a reviewer, who may quote brief passages in a review.

Certain photographs used in this publication are used by license or permission from the owner thereof, or are otherwise publicly available. This publication is not endorsed by any person or entity appearing herein. Any product names, logos, brands or trademarks featured or referred to in the publication are the property of their respective trademark owners. Media Lab Books is not affiliated with, nor sponsored or endorsed by, any of the persons, entities, product names, logos, brands or other trademarks featured or referred to in any of its publications.

ISBN-10: 1-942556-04-7
ISBN-13: 978-1-942556-04-6

CEO Tony Romando
Vice President of Sales and New Markets Tom Mifsud
Vice President of Brand Marketing Joy Bomba
Director of Finance Vandana Patel
Manufacturing Director Nancy Puskuldjian

Editor-in-Chief Jeff Ashworth
Creative Director Steven Charny **Photo Director** Dave Weiss
Content Editor Bailey Bryant
Issue Designer Elizabeth Neal
Issue Photo Editor Lindsay Pogash

Senior Editor James Ellis
Managing Editor Courtney Kerrigan
Associate Editor Tim Baker
Copy Editor Holland Baker
Assistant Editors Bailey Bryant, Trevor Courneen, Alicia Kort
Editorial Assistants Amanda Jaguden, Sarah Kim, Mara Leighton

Photo Editor Meg Reinhardt
Photo Assistant Kelsey Pillischer
Senior Designer Bryn Waryan
Designer Michelle Lock
Design Assistant Nick Harran
Junior Analyst Matthew Quinn

Co-Founders Bob Lee, Tony Romando

Indexing by R studio T, NYC

ALL PHOTOS BY SIMPLY GLUTEN FREE INC. EXCEPT: iStock: p8, 11, 12. Shutterstock: p15.